The Furthest and Nearest Night Stars:

The Birth of The Night Star ☼ + ☽ = *

Second Edition

Autographed

BSPC Global Corporation
DBA
Burnt Store Publishers,
Hosting and Publishing
600 E Seltice Way Ste A PMB 2018
Post Falls, Idaho, 83854

EFS Global Corporation,
DBA
Eating For "SELF," ™
DBA
True Life Poet
Publishing, Sales and Services
2600 E Seltice Way Ste A PMB 2013
Post Falls, Idaho, 83854

Equational Poetry ™ LLC,
Online Sales Agency
30 N Gould St Ste R
Sheridan, WY 82801

The Furthest ☼ and Nearest ☽ Night Stars: The Birth of The Night Star * Second Edition Autographed dedication is to my Filipino family, and beautiful wife Nelfa whose November 21, birthday or March 8 wedding anniversary will never be forgotten, as they are now written WITHIN the stars.

The Furthest and Nearest Night Stars: The Birth of "The Night Star" * Second Edition paperback would NOT have materialized WITHOUT Nelfa's undying "True Love" *♥ΨΧΔ and support?

*♥ΨΧΔ – **"True Love"** ♂

☽♠ΨΧΔ – **"Taboo Love"** ♂

☽♣ΨΧΔ – **"'SELF'- Pity Love"** (form of regret) ♂

☽♦ΨΧΔ – **"Trophy Love"** ♂

See The Black Hill's Time Capsule "Story," The "Story" WITHIN a "Story," Book IV of The Domestic marine ® Tandem Book Writing and "Equational" and Engendered Poetry Series with parallel and recursive writing, for masculine "True Love:" ♂ – The Allegory of The Apple.

See The Allegory of The Apple Extension for feminine "True Love:" ♀

The Soul requires masculine ♂ and feminine ♀ "True Love" in transformations of conflations for completion.

Middle Eastern leaders have said it, that is, women are NOT human.

"Equational Poetry" ™ derives, a soul does NOT make one human, but rather, ONLY makes it possible TO BE one.

The soul separates man from animal but TO BE human is a whole different configuration.

– Just as sexual intercourse has absolutely NOTHING to do with "True Love," today, that is. --

Today, sex is a response to an agitant. induced by Societal War. If one wants to call a response to an agitant an expression of "True Love" then don't ask why your marriage failed?

In truth, as ONLY one percent of the planet's population holds all the wealth, about the same percentage of people on this planet today can still be considered human. The rest of us losers MORE closely resemble machines. Thank Sigmund Freud, BIG Pharma and commercialization and go recharge.

Those people most closely resembling humans today are people like the Sioux, Bajo, Mongols, Guineans, for example.

An expression of "True Love" in the bedroom in the old world was a ritual that makes what YOU machines do today NOTHING short of sin.

A woman's innate, NON blank slate is like an autopilot for propagation of the species, but NOT meant to progress unchecked. This autopilot is NOT found

WITHIN her soul, does NOT make her human, but rather, provides her purpose beyond her "SELF."

Purpose beyond one's "SELF" is an autopilot and fail-safe for the nurturer of the nuclear family. Her autopilot is kept in check by "True Love" which grounds the nurturer with "SELF" purpose.

In this regard, the nurturer MUST be cared for while her autopilot purpose grounded with "SELF"-purpose, to reach "True Enlightenment."

So, why isn't a nurturer's autopilot and fail-safe purpose meant to go unchecked?

It's unprincipled, that's why!

There is absolutely NOTHING MORE important to humanity than "SELF"-purpose!

Purpose beyond one's "SELF" was ONLY extended to the mother for crisis but was all WAYs meant TO BE kept in check by "True Love."

A woman will do anything for her children in times of crisis which amounts to insanity, foolishness, irresponsibility and even evil. Thus, jeopardizing the nuclear family.

"Equational Poetry" ™ derives that it's NOT intelligence that separates us from the animals. Moreover, "True" intelligence would keep us connected with our environments?

What separates us from the animals are the same things that are meant to keep us connected with our environments, those are, moral components.

Therefore, the reason God gave Satan a tail is because Satan can NOT be MORE than an animal because NOTHING Satan does contains a moral component, but yet Satan is childishly intelligent.

The conclusion is that the wealthier one is the MORE childish their intelligence and MORE of an animal that they become, eventually growing a tail and joining Satan.

Hence, as Renee Descartes proclaimed, "I think therefore I am," does NOT confirm a human, unless or until their thinking maintains moral components, which politics and money prevents.

Even of a child's age, I thought, what an utterly simplistic thing to say! How could this seemingly simplistic utterance have any kind of relevance?

Well, whatever people saw me as my whole life, whether a poor, unappealing, unpopular kid from a dysfunctional family with the wrong last name or a disabled Veteran with issues, I did not become what those people saw! I became who I am! It wasn't so simple after all, but now "I see, therefore I believe," and now I understand, that "I think, therefore I am!"

For those that are not interested in my life, then consider buying the books for the recipes or the health info? Who knows, maybe they will save a "True Life?"

Since the first of its kind and its original literary work, that came first, of the very first Tandem Book Writing Series, materialized the REFERENCE MANUAL, "Equational Poetry," ™ to complete the series, the REFERENCE MANUAL was compelled to return the favor by materializing The Tandem Poetry Series.

Book 1 of The Tandem Poetry Series is NOT the REFERENCE MANUAL, but rather, the 1ˢᵗ book WITHIN THE POETRIES-PRIOR entitled Equational Poetry, ™ the same title as the REFERENCE MANUAL but NOT the same book.

--Don't forget that everyday is Sunday in the cabin, in the wildlife preserve, remember?--

When God created heaven and earth and man in his own image, it would be silly to think that he had a feminine image of him "SELF?"

It would also be foolish to believe that he did NOT devise the method of reproduction before his own image.

This is why "WE" all begin WITHIN the feminine before the male asserts him "SELF."

The entire "Story" of Adam and Eve can be interpreted as symbolic but remains irrelevant either WAY, however, the "True" symbolism of the "Story" of Adam and Eve that shall all WAYs remain relevant is the symbolism of woman coming from the rib of man because forgetting this symbolism is what devolves the Y chromosome out of existence.

Introduction to The POETRIES-PRIOR and The Tandem Poetry Series!

The 4 "Story's" in "True Life"…The POETRIES-PRIOR or Pre-"First Philosophy" to the origin of mathematics, music, magic, art and beyond.

Poetries   Poetry   POETRIES-PRIOR

Understanding the Narratives We Live By

The Personal "Story:" Crafting Your Individual Journey, the concept of the personal "Story" is integral to understanding how individuals perceive and navigate their lives. Each person crafts a unique narrative that encapsulates their experiences, choices,…

Pulse Poetry

Of the Tandem Poetry Series, "Picture Paintings" Poetry is getting the most attention. "Equational Poetry" ™ analysis derives because "Picture Paintings" Poetry is the pulse of The Tandem Poetries. — "It's what the heart makes, NOT wants?"…

Side Note: Septagram "According to the Greek Alphabet Code, letters of the Ancient Greek Alphabet reach out to our present times modified or 'deformed', compared to their original form, but they continue to 'carry' meanings."

. . .

. . .

"...describes the operations and functions of Nature and that's what makes it Immortal..."

. . .

. . .

"...all this knowledge that connects Art with Nature, sprang alive in front of my eyes.

All of a sudden, the letters have been converted to 'deograms', that not only they had (according to the Code) a univocal meaning-interpretation,..."

. . .

. . .

Language is a living organism

"Taking into consideration that language is a living organism, we could imagine that it has 'flesh and bones'. This part of 'bones', which is the main structure of a word and the basis of its meaning, is played by the consonants. So the part of the 'flesh', which is the voice and the light of the word, is played by the vowels.

The Greek Language has more vowels than any other language, so, when talking in Greek, we emit more light, using a range of 7 colors. We hear 7 musical notes, we see 7 colors, we have 7 energy centers and the vowels of the Greek Alphabet are 7."

. . .

. . .

"The human body is structured according to Nature and the physical Laws of our planet. So when we consciously use a language that reflects and obeys these Laws, we live in better terms with each other and our environment, we become cleverer, and we walk the highway of Philosophy, mother of all sciences, no matter what's the educational level of each, which is a road to improvement of a person, from human to 'Anthropos'".

"In my opinion, the Greek Language is the Solar Language that enlightens people's minds. You don't need to be a Greek citizen or to have been born in a country called Greece, to be ΕΛΛΗΝ. Every seeker of the Truth on this planet, using his logic, has the potential to become ΕΛΛΗΝ."

– The Greek Reporter

The ACES "ofLoves," ♥♣♦♠ the 2017 total eclipse of the sun and the first "Picture Painting" realized at Koreshan State Park in 2018 materializing the "NIGHT STAR," * "True Love" and the origin of mathematics illuminated the idea of "Equational Poetry" ™ mathematical symbols.

I have to confess that she was my first "True Love." *♥ΨXΔ

Literized [structured] original literature WITHIN the realm of truth in learning, health and [wholistic] wellness.

*♥ΨXΔ is an "Equational Poetry" ™ expression of "True Love." – An expression is NOT an equation.

The History of math is now extended.

Koreshan State Park

Furthermore, The Aces "ofLoves" ♥♣♦♠ Heart ♥ and Spade ♠ were previously disclosed, below the ACES "ofLoves" ♥♣♦♠ Club ♣ and Diamond ♦ are disclosed.

The symbols WITHIN the expression of "True Love" are modern day representations for familiarity's sake. However, Ronda, Burnt Store Publisher's sketch artist, is sketching the definitive "Equational Poetry" ™ companion derivative symbols of the expression of "True Love" defined by The goddess of "True Love."

What does it mean TO BE literized?

literized.com

The first of its kind scope, realm, structure, content and "SELF" WITHIN truth in learning, health and [wholistic} wellness.

Literized original literature. —

Scope *

Realm ♥

Structure Ψ

Content X

"SELF" Δ

. . .

. . .

When the door open, the old was born again, thus, a "Picture Painting" is an old image re-imagined with new meaning?

Images have always been WITHIN the heavens, an image is a picture is distinct from a painting in that the picture's meaning is held WITHIN the picture's painting?

The first "Picture Painting," that is, The "Night Star," * holds the image and the meaning for the born again Christian.

A Christian can be born again and again with each "Picture Painting" of an old image re-imagined with new meaning?

Your first ABSTRACT work represents one-sided "True Love" reentering God's earthly world like a carpenter that's sent to collect materials to complete one's home in "SELF"-sonder.

YOU and your entire existence as a living and commercial entity are for the sole purpose of riding our backs to the black hole of hell. I buck YOU off here.

* Literized [nakabalangkas] orihinal na panitikan sa loob ng larangan ng katotohanan sa pag-aaral, kalusugan at [wholistic] kagalingan. *♥ΨXΔ ay ang pagpapahayag ng "Tunay na Pag-ibig" ng "Equational Poetry." ™ - Ang isang ekspresyon ay HINDI isang equation. Sa ngayon, ang kasaysayan ng matematika ay pinalawak. Koreshan State Park Bukod dito, ang The Aces "ofLoves" ♥♣♦♠ Heart ♥ and Spade ♠ ay nauna nang inihayag, gayunpaman, Ang Pinakamalayo * at Pinakamalapit * na Mga Bituin sa Gabi: Ang Kapanganakan ng "Night Star," * paperback Second Edition na darating sa Hulyo sa kauna-unahang pagkakataon ay nagbubunyag ng ACES "ofLoves" Club ♣ at Diamond ♦. Ang mga nabanggit na simbolo sa loob ng ekspresyon ng "Tunay na Pag-ibig" ay mga modernong representasyon para sa kapakanan ng pamilyar. Gayunpaman, binabalangkas ni Ronda ang tiyak na "Equational Poetry" ™ na kasamang mga simbolo ng nabanggit na ekspresyon ng "Tunay na Pag-ibig" na tinukoy ng diyosa ng "Tunay na Pag-ibig."

"Equational Poetry" ™ chose the word "packed" presently for the Filipino translation, YOU see? That is, a Satan Tree, producing an antonym to

The POETRIES.

This so-called study moves to the issue of children raising children, which sheds a spotlight on Microsoft as a NON value added company from its inception. "New data shows why players quit—and what you can do about it? Latency doesn't just frustrate players—it drives them away. Our latest study found that 78% of gamers have rage quit mid-session due to lag. For studios and developers, that means every second of server delay can translate to lost users, bad reviews, and lower lifetime value."

. . .

. . .

At the turn of the 20th century, Washington DC had an opportunity to use Anti trust legislation to take the United States and the nuclear family in a quite different direction. However, beginning with BIG "SUGAR", the United State's supreme court decided to screw the nation, the family and the world by forming a packed with Satan

Just as road rage is a real concern, video game rage destroys relationships and families. Government, corporate and the religious need TO BE put in their places while mothers and fathers need to take back their families and "True Lifes!"

There's NO doubt that the bible has been altered throughout the Time-Tolls by the wealthy, by kings, by clergy and others for their own personal gain. The feminist uses this fact for her own personal gain rather than try to understand it?

Moreover, words of yesteryear held ABSTRACTIONS lost in translation or reinterpretation, such as, the word SUBMISSION?

The Feminist calls SUBMISSION, CHAUVINISM, and uses it as a political weapon. The Feminist wants TO BE on top and in control of every situation, but how does one control SUBMISSION, desire?

"Equational Poetry" ™ finds the Feminist deliberate, all WAYS operating WITHIN a CONTEXT.

A "True" woman has desires, and also sometimes requires? She requires friendship, companionship, strength, comfort WITHOUT any CONTEXT. Her CONTEXT is lost WITHIN trust, "True Love" and commitment.

A "True" wife's CONTEXT-less moments WITHIN a truly loving relationship with her husband are when she SUBMITS to her own desires to the ONLY man that can fulfill them, that's NOT CHAUVINISM.

Border of boundaries

"True Love" is NOT the end; it's the beginning.

The materialization of "True Love" does NOT mean one will never love again. On the contrary, materializing "True Love" is just the beginning of a reordering "ofLove."

The materialization of "True Love" forms a border of boundaries beneath it, NOT limitations "ofLove," while above "True Love," one shall find NOTHING but God's pure love.

The man and woman of "True Love" are NO longer afraid "ofLove." Their strength is WITHIN their focus above on NOTHING but God's pure love.

Their focus above keeps out what's below to grow WITHIN its own boundaries "ofLove."

What's below others "True Love" that attempts to cross its boundary above, meet with OLEP who offers a new quest "ofLove."

If it comes back from its quest and still attempts to cross its boundary above, Genie Magician is there to offer a shuffle "ofLove?"

If it's dealt the Joker of Freedom from "ofLove" by Genie Magician, The goddess of "True Love" surfaces from a splash above to examine its one-sided "True Love."

YOU may NOT recall, *"The any 9 miles canyon walk?"* It is a story that I perceived and moralized while conquering the Santa Monica Mountain range and Malibu Canyon area while hiding like a criminal in the woods in the Calibasis area an area where government supposedly made it impossible for one to survive outdoors and impossible NOT TO BE discovered? I lived in the woods for 2 months before making my WAY to LA.

"The any 9 miles canyon walk" is a story, because of its brevity. However, I'm expanding the story into an allegory?

In any case, *"The any 9 miles canyon walk"* holds a moral of intrinsic value. Intrinsic value came to mind while at the Gaisano Mall today, in Iligan City, Philippines.

I found very little of what are termed products and services at the Gaisano Mall that hold intrinsic value.

Moreover, the objection to the microwave oven is also about a lack of intrinsic value.

All manufactured products today that are shipped to the Philippines hold NO intrinsic value. They are to create lifelong ignorant customers and consumers through forced and limited options while eliminating *"True"* choice. They are to destroy *"SELF,"* *"True Life"* and the natural world around us, making the rich richer and the poor poorer. Remember that the definition of wealth and riches in this make-believe manufactured world that *"WE"* are forced to exist in is ownership of manufactured material possessions and money, neither of which hold intrinsic value. The rich are the ignorant while the masses have resorted to stupidity for petty pleasures and addictions instead of intrinsic value of the liberal arts and Renaissance.

Santa Monica Mountains

Malibu Creek

Keeping the Faith

"Equational Poetry" ™ *materialized from a "Picture Painting," YOU SEE? The "Picture Painting" materialized by its and my "SELF" recursively, indeed, 1 + 1 = 3, or MORE, confirmed by The "Night Star!" **

The "Night Star," * the first "PICTURE-PAINTING," confirmed that schooling is for slaves while Education is a QUEST for "True Enlightenment."

The POETRIES and THE POETRIES-PRIOR or PRE-"FIRST-PHILOSOPHY" framework began with "EQUATIONAL POETRY" ™ but grew into The TANDEM POETRY SERIES, its COMPANION and EXTENSION, HISTORY in the making.

The "'NEW' math" in the 60s and 70s, leading to The Digital Transformation, including The UNIT CIRCLE and IMAGINARY NUMBERS is a scam and oppression like the smartphone is a weapon of mass destruction, but there is still a Time-Toll to catch-up to religious, scientific, governmental, and corporate nonsense and surpass as well as overcome it regardless of any others resolve, with "True Life" mathematics and "True Enlightenment."
– Keeping the Faith!

The Hippocratic Oath

People die needlessly each and everyday because of religion, science, government, corporate, doctors, lawyers but also because of their own greed, laziness and stupidity.

I spared YOU the addiction because I'm compassionate enough to blame addiction on science and government, industry, greed but YOU must own your own greed, laziness and stupidity.

YOU allow the fools, incompetent, the evil to rule YOU because it's easier than facing the truth. YOU rather die than put-up a fight.

Again, like work, does NOT mean a 9 to 5 job, but rather, a struggle for a principled "True Life?"

Tossing-out your "SELF" for easy, animal byproducts, coffee, cheese, pizza, blended oils, chocolate, candy, donuts, is like tossing-out the baby with the bath water or jumping from the frying pan to the fire, WITHOUT the 3rd flame of passion?

To exist for NOTHING MORE than eating, what the hell do YOU expect?

Human beings are NOT meant to drink or eat cow's milk but many can't go a day WITHOUT it?

Doctors claim that their patience refuse to follow their wholistic approach to cure, so the doctors comply with BIG Pharma to keep their penthouses and expensive cars, expensive husbands and expensive wives.

The Hippocratic Oath says, do NO harm, but since their patience want to die any WAY, they choose the money?

One can't blame evil for doing what it's suppose to do, but what about good people that choose death rather than giving-up McDonald's, oils, all purpose flour?

Reassembling that which is broken

The youth, especially of today, but it's most of any age, that is, their aspirations are those of sitting on their asses and being waited upon.

Most today accept their imprisonments with pleasure going NO where. They are comforted by the thought of doing NOTHING verses the thought of working for a true living.

This attitude, like following the money carrot off the cliff, will eventually bite them on the ass.

The feminist, wealthy, religious, scientist, government, industry will accept NOTHING less than a worthless existence of spending others money.

However, "Equational Poetry" ™ concurs with Engendered Poetry's assertion and the age-old adage of "idle hands are the devil's workshop."

"'Working' for a true living" has taken on yet another English deceptive connotation making everyone, especially the youth, terrified of working. However, again, "Equational Poetry" ™ finds that "True Life" all WAYs was and all WAYs shall be work, WITHOUT the added notion of a job.

The Wise Old Owl of the Forest told OLEP that a kept human being is equivalent to a slave, while the comfort of home today represents a prison.

The satisfaction of materializing from the Heart, Mind, Soul, "SELF" is the work and pleasure of a true human.

Jesus was a carpenter who reassembled Hearts, Minds, Souls, "SELFs", NOT built. Building is NOT what humans are meant to do but rather reassemble that which is broken.

Pouring concrete across the earth, blocking the wind with buildings, polluting the earth, wind and water shall ONLY bring us closer to the edge of the black hole of hell.

All children today grow-up to wonder where was and what was my childhood? The goal of every human being is the aspiration of growth, development, "True Enlightenment," "True Love," ascension beyond.

The ONLY WAY to reach any of that is to get off your ass, and place your mental abilities on reassembling that which is broken.

Understanding The POETRIES-PRIOR, Pre-"'First Philosophy,'" YOU SEE?

Say hello to The "True Life" POET. — What YOU see is what YOU get if grown from the seed of "Equational Poetry?" ™

Explaining "PROSPERITY," war, the industrial revolution, nuclear war, the digital transformation, lost civilizations and the lost generation. The POETRIES-PRIOR or Pre-"First Philosophy" to the origin of mathematics, music, magic, art and beyond.

The Tandem Poetry Series and Its Metaphysical Foundations: A Deep Dive into "First Philosophy:"

Understanding "First Philosophy" and Its Metaphysical Roots.

"First philosophy" seeks to address questions about the essence of being and the fundamental structure of reality. Core concepts in metaphysics include ontology, epistemology, cosmology and now "Equational Poetry." ™

The Tandem Poetry Series represents a unique confluence of literary artistry and philosophical inquiry, offering a new lens through which to examine age-old metaphysical questions.

Originating in the early 2000s, the series was the brainchild of Richard Jon Hassey, The "True Life" Poet, and Hassey's "Equational Poetry" ™ *pre "First-philosophy" that seeks to explore the intersections between poetic expression and* metaphysical thought with works that deftly navigate the complexities of existence and the nature of "SELF."

At its core, the Tandem Poetry Series uses poetry as a medium to probe metaphysical questions, providing an alternative to traditional philosophical discourse. The series posits that poetry, with its evocative language and capacity for nuance, can offer profound insights into the nature of reality and our place WITHIN it. This approach allows for a more intuitive and emotional engagement with metaphysical themes, making complex philosophical concepts more accessible to a broader audience.

One notable example WITHIN the series is the poem "True Beauty," which contemplates the delicate balance between the physical and metaphysical realms. Through "Picture Painting's" imagery and contemplative tone, Hassey explores the interconnectedness of all things, prompting readers to reflect on their own existence and the larger cosmic order. Similarly, "Equational Poetry," ™ loosely termed Book V, The Reference Manual to The Domestic marine ® Tandem Book Writing and "Equational" and Engendered Poetry Series with parallel and recursive writing, delves into the concept of the "SELF," questioning the boundaries between individual identity and the universal experience.

POETRY has all WAYS been defined WITHIN a SINGULARITY throughout "FIRST PHILOSOPHY," *just like love, but "Equational Poetry"* ™ *derived POETRY and LOVE PLURALITIES, YOU see?*

  See The Black Hill's Time Capsule "Story," The "Story" WITHIN a "Story," Book IV of The Domestic marine ® *Tandem Book Writing and "Equational" and Engendered Poetry Series with parallel and recursive writing, for masculine "True Love:"* ♂

Aces "ofLoves" ♥♣♦♠ *– The Allegory of The Apple.*

See The Allegory of The Apple Extension for feminine "True Love:" ♀ *Art "ofLoves."*

Any opinions expressed in this book or series do NOT represent the official positions of the U.S. Department of the Navy or any of its associates?

Preface

What you're about to read here are insights into my book entitled **The Furthest** ☼ **and Nearest** ☽ **Night Stars: The Birth of** "The Night Star." * **Second Edition** --Book II of The Domestic marine ® Tandem Book Writing and "Equational" and Engendered Poetry Series with parallel and recursive writing. The main book's, The Domestic marine ®: Never Before and Never Again; there is only one "Domestic marine," companion book.

One may find it interesting to note that these two books were written in parallel with one another while at the same Time-Toll engaging social media. Much of the information in these books were written to social media before or at the same Time-Toll that the information were written WITHIN the books.

There are many MORE details on the truth and additional information that have NOT been disclosed to the public throughout the chapters and series(s). Furthermore, the books are much MORE than a semi autobiography. The books have new ideas, health information, computer science and programming information, vegan recipes, herbal remedies, relationship information and advice, and much MORE.

This book mentions virtual reality, online dating, social media and dating and getting back to the basics when it comes to relationships, especially for the Millennial! -- Virtual reality is what inspired the companion book, along with social media and my online encounter with my Tomboy first love from childhood. – A Tomboy in the United States is NOT a homosexual as one is in the Philippines.

The main book is MORE informational (Informative – earthly truths). First "True Life" events remain chronological and sequential, while WITHIN the companion book, first "True Life" events do NOT remain sequential and are NOT necessarily chronological.

The companion book is MORE relational (Relationships – spiritual guidance) and is meant to share most significant and beneficial events and encounters that have the most potential to effect positive change in relationships and society, mitigating the devastating results of The Societal War that evolved from The Cold War that never truly ended.

Why did the architect that desecrated the Sioux nation's black hill's put Roosevelt's head before Lincoln's on "Mount Rushmore?"

Don't believe them and don't forget that Genie Magician is The Angel One's counterpart in Book IV.

The Angel One NOT ONLY works for Aphrodite but is her prize pupil as The Grape Fairy is OLEP's.

Who'd a guest that The Angel One could get MORE from Code Talker Poker than the ACE "ofLove's" club offered?

The ACE "ofLove's" diamond brought the Feminist WITHIN a man's game. OH MY, the "BIG Bang" theory of homosexuality began!

Vietnam was needed PRIOR to the mafia offing JFK, because the government takeover gave the American people constitutional rights to take-back their government, but Selective Service took care of that!

The "REBIRTH of AMERICA," after JFK's murder, was WITHIN the secular.

As the last citizen of the lost generation, my first "True Life" ended at age 50, for several reasons, one being The "Greatest Generation's" efforts to find and acknowledge me, YOU see?

The Furthest ☼ and Nearest ☽ Night Stars: The Birth of "The Night Star" * is symbolic of, NOT just the end of my first "True Life," but the beginning of my second.

America was reborn WITHIN the secular after offing JFK, and, while, though my first "True Life" remained WITHIN the spiritual, it was deplete of "True Love."

However, my second "True Life" had a rebirth 4 years after it began, remaining WITHIN the spiritual but now, full of "True Love."

It was this one-sided rebirth of "True Love" that conflated to completion with Nelfa's undying one-sided "True Love."

. . .

. . .

2024 post: You're mistaken. Those are the thoughts of a woman, that is, one that believes in abortion, and that their children are their property, which makes them a Feminist hypocrite, for I was alive the day JFK died. I just wasn't born yet.

My birthday is 12/30/1963, and for your information, in this Information Age, that makes information a commodity and MORE valuable than money, especially your Fiat money that the Black Hill's Gold Standard was rendered for jewelry and industry, which is another example of what is NOT "TRUE" Capitalism, or "TRUE" "sustainability," I have recalled memories from when I was WITHIN my mother's womb.

WITHIN my semi-autobiography, I mention some of my earliest of a child's age memories. The recalled memories PRIOR to those that are already written and published, that is, PRIOR to pre, pre-kindergarten are saved for The Domestic marine: CORE, PART 2, completing my autobiography and yet another book series.

Decided to add sub chapters to some chapters. Between many chapters are short sub chapters, examining topics of particular interest MORE closely.

The first sub chapter WITHIN this book is called **Sub Chapter 2 – Getting to The Heart ♥ of The Matter**.

Each chapter is like a mini book in and of its "SELF," satisfying, but the reader wanting MORE, so each of the following chapters is progressively satisfying to the reader and each books focus remains on the thesis of the series(s).

Thesis: *"You can't change the past but I'll be damned if I'm going to let it define me!"*

". . . ..was up late again, been waking up in the middle of the night lately and jotting down some thoughts."

This is a part of the "Story" of my first "True Life."

As Time-Toll progresses in these "Stories," "pause" is occasionally taken to relay MORE detailed information on topics of particular interest, again, for the reader's sake.

No one's name, but perhaps, where unavoidable, is used for my own principled reasons, NOT necessarily to protect the parties involved?

It was Benjamin Franklin that invented the bifocal because he was the first to recognize that distinctions could be brought together and the distinction's proximity were beneficial.

However, there was a clear and easily recognizable difference between the distinctions. – Each of the tops of the glasses' lenses were for seeing clearer at a distance while each of the bottoms of the lenses were for seeing clearer up close, for reading, that he did much of the time.

Benjamin Franklin was unaware of it at the time and did not recognize that he also engaged in "Tandem Seeing," as a function of his bifocal invention?

"Tandem Seeing" is "Tandem Book Writing's" source of distinctions!

I did not invent "Tandem Seeing" nor did Benjamin Franklin! He invented bifocals that allowed him to engage in "Tandem Seeing!" "Tandem Seeing" is not an invention, it has always been around us but never recognized or discovered until now!

The discovery of "Tandem Seeing" made recognizable by Benjamin Franklin's bifocal invention led to today's invention of "Tandem Book Writing!" Therefore, the recognition of "Tandem Seeing" brought about the invention of "Tandem Book Writing."

Hence, discoveries are just as important as inventions and the world is out there to discover, new things everyday because the world is constantly changing. This fact is another reason why "True Love" was necessary to be a constant in the universe, to make sure that there were always distinctions to bring together, to form new sources of discoveries.

Therefore, the science of optics made "True Love" more recognizable, but today, science has gone too far, e.g. as with the "invisiline" bifocal.

The "invisiline" bifocal removed the distinction between the lenses and thus prevents "Tandem Seeing" and makes "True Love" less recognizable.

My term for science going too far and eliminating distinctions is called an "Invisilife."

Science, in and of itself, is not at fault as shown, science made "True Love" more recognizable, however, when profit becomes the only motivation instead of "Personal Evolution" and discovery of the "True World" around us, distinctions are inevitably lost and thus, "True Love" becomes less recognizable!

This is where we're heading with "Virtual Reality," no more distinctions, no more discovery, no more "True World," no more "True Life," no more "True Love!" –"Invisilife!"

without the prior written permission of Richard Jon Hassey.

Review search engine appearance

Make sure the title and summary that appear when people find your website on search engines are accurate and appealing.

Search result preview

Discover the Invisilife Children's Book Series | Truth in Learning

https://www.invisiliferevealed.com/

Explore the Invisilife children's book series that promotes truth in learning, health, and wellness through "SELF"-reliance. Get the Invisilife Revealed student notebook, part of the series by Richard Jon Hassey and Nelfa Salise Hassey...

Updated Jun 23, 2025 4:09:40 am

Finally, the depth of the insights presented here is kept at a level so as to be MORE appealing to a wider audience and hopefully draw you, the reader, WITHIN an intense and engaging reading experience!

Once again, the focus remains on the thesis of the series(s):

Thesis: *"You can't change the past but I'll be damned if I'm going to let it define me!"*

Let's begin

The Furthest and Nearest Night Stars:

The Birth of The Night Star * Second Edition
(Total eclipse of the sun, 2017) ☼ + ☽ = *

To my Tomboy friend and The Angel One who made my insurmountable goal obtainable in a relatively short period of Time-Toll WITHIN their insincerity.

Chapter 1 – Early Childhood

With most children, suspect, life starts out in wonder, curiosity and a sense of fair play, that is, until the social interactions with others begins!

Beginning of The Domestic marine ® overlap.

Looking back on my early childhood, it's quite easy to see now that as early as pre-K, was put into situations that demanded responsibility.

With that, My mother is divorced, since I was three years old, so don't really know my father . . . sibling rivalries; common place, dysfunctions in family structure develop and notice that my mother is telling me about her day MORE-so then she is telling my brothers and sisters. – I'm the youngest boy of three and have three sisters, one a year younger.

Believe that this dysfunction is what lead to reading books . . . read a little pocket bible in bed and later started reading a book about electronics from one of my uncles.

Remember trying to figure out the color codes on resisters. These are some of my earliest memories but prior to this Time-Toll, as just mentioned, do have memories of head-start, kindergarten and elementary school.

In the fifth grade, will never forget, the home room teacher burst into the classroom shouting: "It's your fault that Miss. B died because you gave her such a hard time in class." Coincidentally or NOT, she looked right at me when she said it!

-- I Joked around in music class MORE than anyone else because what was being taught seemed TO BE ridiculous to me?

Have two points to be made here, one, the home room teacher scarred a lot of children for life with her totally unacceptable emotional rant of nonsense and two, much subject-matter taught in pre-K to post secondary education is based on antiquated systems that have been passed down generation after generation that can hardly be interpreted by anyone but like-minded individuals?

Just because someone simply doesn't think like Bach or Beethoven doesn't mean that they are NOT intelligent or can't design their own music system that makes MORE sense to the majority of people?

Along the same lines as when Microsoft ® stole CP/M's commands and claimed them their work for hire, while under contract with IBM, ® then stealing the concept of Windows ® from Steve Jobs to make DOS ® easier to use once the mouse was on the horizon and the list of commands became too long for people to remember so with Windows ® and a mouse one wouldn't have to remember and type cryptic commands at a command prompt; just run a command or MACRO from a menu system with the click of a mouse?

Do NOT believe the modern day write-ups on the early days of DOS, ® because, like the Windows 98 ® government "antitrust lawsuit," which was a government takeover of Microsoft, ® the government supported Bill Gates in the early days as a stooge, and played him like they played Trump.

CP/M was the first "True" DOS, but like the barcode, was waiting for the end of the unconstitutional Vietnam War, which was unofficially 1974. There is NO coincidence in "Equational Poetry" ™ backwards extrapolation.

While attending the Edison Community College Collier Branch in Naples, Florida back in the 1980's, met the guys that invented the mouse.

Point being, backwards compatibility of Microsoft ® Windows ® Operating Systems led to less than elegant products. Microsoft ® should have started over with scratch long ago but we are all forced to learn the system that is in place as inefficient as it has become. There must be a better way!

During physics class, in 2001, often wondered how bright a person to describe the creation of our universe with such "eloquent" a theory as "The Big Bang Theory?" "Genius?" NOT to mention, "Dark Matter!" "Brilliant?"

We are all forced with learning the world around us as described by "others!" –Like-minded individuals! Well, I'm hoping to keep you drawn into an intense and engaging reading experience because I'm redefining my "SELF" on my own terms for a change and would like to help you do the same? You won't want to miss it, keep reading!

To continue the engagement with computer science and programming, physics and Albert Einstein, -- the paid and endorsed SYMBOL of "AMERICAN Intelligence," -- please refer to The Silencer Project's companion book: The Poker Game Algorithm and The Tandem Book Writing Reference Manual, loosely termed, Book V of the original series, entitled: "Equational Poetry," ™ NOT TO BE confused with the first book WITHIN The Tandem Poetry Series.

Some later memories were of my teddy bears. – NOT sure where the one that use too "beat-up" came from but the other one, I'll never forget, the grandma, on my mother's side. The reason that I'll never forget this teddy bear is because my brother grabbed it from me one night and said: "You're too old for this now" and he threw it into our coal furnace . . . immediately started crying! Incidentally, we were the only ones on the street who still had a coal furnace.

Shortly after running up stairs my brother followed; asked him, "could we go get the teddy bear out of the furnace? . . . ..if there are any burnt spots on him, we could cut them off with a pair of scissors."

When we went back down to the cellar and he opened the coal furnace door, all that I saw was the silhouette of my teddy bear that my grandma gave me in ashes . . . ran back upstairs crying again.

. . . cried for several days afterward. (NOT at the Time-Toll but now realize that it was the link to my grandma, NOT the loss of the teddy bear that was upsetting to me). –My grandma died of breast cancer in the early nineteen seventies.

. . . after losing the teddy bear, started having nightmares and running down stairs after midnight in a panic. These nightmares went on for years and were of my grandma. Never told anyone about these events. (These nightmares, . . . my subconscious reconnects with my grandma in replace of the teddy bear).

This is the moment in my first "True Life," after suffering this loss and realizing how much pain that loss can cause while recognizing how much that I was depended on that I developed a keen and exceptional sense of humor and subconsciously vowed to be the one that everyone could depend on to prevent or ease this type of pain.

My Teddy bear was the first "lose" that I suffered in my first "True Life;" as SYMBOLIC as it was, it was real for me, subconsciously! –This is when truly lost my grandma WITHIN me!

End of The Domestic marine ® overlap.

Compounding things even MORE was the truth that was in a single parent home while bonding with my grandfather had already occurred (mature mentality) prior to my grandma's death. My mother continued to rely on me MORE and MORE for emotional support.

Additionally, due to the truth that my brothers were heading down the wrong rebellious path, for typical broken home reasons, my mother made me her "pet project" to make sure of . . . NOT going down the same path brothers chose.

My mother focused on raising me as the type of man that she expected of me but her upbringing was dysfunctional too. What were my mother's expectations for raising the perfect man?

Looking back on some of the events in my early childhood now, it seemed that had a relatively tough Time-Toll of it but back then it seemed normal?

. . . . .some neighborhood friends that spent a lot of Time-Toll with . . . liked to play football with them especially.

One of my friends was a "Tomboy," which in the United States is NOT a homosexual like in the Philippines, and I have to confess that she was my first "True Love." *♥ΨXΔ "True," in the sense, the love was real for me and as it was developing honestly believed that she developed the same for me.

*♥ΨXΔ is an "Equational Poetry" ™ expression of "True Love." An expression is NOT an equation.

The History of math is now extended.

My memories are clear on this matter, let me take a "pause" now to explain some thoughts, feelings and emotions, again, for the reader's sake:

My friends and I spent much Time-Toll together as children before graduating from high school . . . can't mention every encounter or this book would be too long?

There was a significant moment between me and my first love however. While playing outside and falling down together, she landed a top of me. She would NOT get up for an awkward amount of Time-Toll and when she did, my other friends even asked, "what was that all about?"

This is when our relationship or lack thereof changed.

She began to pull away from me anyTime-Toll that I would begin to get close to her, symbolically, physically, or emotionally . . . believe that this event embarrassed her and she was hurt that I didn't respond in some way?

Have to remember that we were very young children and I did NOT have a father to go to with my problems.

After mentioning this event to my mother, my mother dismissed my feelings. -- My mother did NOT believe that anyone was good enough for her "pet project."

Also, believe that my mother, in a WAY, she felt threatened by any potential relationships that I might develop with others because she needed me all to her "SELF."

These events lead to a complex problem and back to explore my previous statement: "What were my mother's expectations for raising the 'perfect man?'"

What was the "perfect man" in her eyes?

It turns out that it was her father! In her attempts to mold me into her expectations of the "perfect man," she shaped me into her father! -- The bonding with my grandpa that I mentioned earlier made my mother's job that much easier.

Remember that at this Time-Toll my mother was NOT even aware of what was occurring. My relationship that was developed with the entire family was that of a "father-figure." –But, one of my sisters resisted this subconscious relationship because she was bitter toward our mother.

These relationship dynamics in the household compounded my relationship dynamics outside the household, as does the dynamics WITHIN others' households similarly do.

In addition, throwing racism, bigotry, nationality, ethnicity, religion, hatred, stereotyping, wealth, poverty, appearance, social status among many other social issues into the mix is a social experiment setup for failure from the start . . . as was another social experiment that I unwittingly participated in after graduating from high school and having the course of my first "True Life" changed forever; that is, until "taking back my first 'True Life'" relatively shortly before beginning the writing of this book.

Please refer to the main book WITHIN the original series, entitled: The Domestic marine ®: Never Before and Never Again; There is ONLY One "Domestic Marine" for MORE detailed explanations.

Carrying this subconscious "father-figure" mentality with me outside the home, (. . . and although had no relationship with my father [he was, to my understanding], half German and half Irish while my mother claimed to be full-blooded Slovak from what is now referred to as the Republic of Slovakia) . . . (My mother's mother was most likely Russian but just as many did NOT claim to be Jewish during the World Wars, many did NOT claim to be Russian during the Cold War that NEVER truly ended, but rather, evolved into The Societal War, solely based on my last name, defined an Irishman growing up?)

That's NOT all, however, bad enough that definition was, I was also from a poor dysfunctional family with brothers that cut a path for me to a dead end.

Therefore, when my first love fell a top of me, NOT responding appropriately, adding to her embarrassment and slightly hurting her compounded with the social issues already mentioned, she dismissed her feelings as easily as my mother dismissed mine.

Furthermore, because my Tomboy friend had an abusive father and poor male role models in her life she chose NOT to get close to me and pulled away from me anyTime-Toll that I started getting too close because she was already "damaged" by the men in her life. She was as accepting of my subconscious "father-figure" mentality as my own family. She needed a "father-figure" in her life as well.

For a significant number of girls and women, once they are hurt by a boy or a man, they bury their thoughts, feelings and emotions so as too never surface again and go through the rest of their lives "damaged," unfeeling toward another man. This circumstance also makes the so called "bad boys" MORE appealing to them for relationships because the girls and women can suppress their feelings MORE easily with these types.

These women take on the pathology that they have to hurt the man first before the man hurts them and this is how these women conduct their lives . . . a toss into the mix an "Irishman" who is/are known for being emotional and there is no quicker end to a caring, feeling, emotional and passion full relationship with some women.

This is also why the Italians typically don't get along with the Irish because a typical Irishman is emotional and just like many others, the Italians don't like to address feelings; they rather have fun, like women.

However, no day gone by in this "Irishman's" first or second "True Life" that every single thought, feeling and emotion that he has encountered hasn't been addressed and dealt with appropriately while mental anguish which can be a major issue in later life is NOT of the slightest concern for this "Irishman."

The older one gets the MORE they will realize that those life-long suppressed memories, thoughts, feelings and emotions will be a major problem for them and ironically that's when an "Irishman" is needed in their lives the most!

My assumed responsibilities to the family continued to grow, along with, NOT ONLY, my "SELF"-imposed "father-figure" role, but my newly acquired, keen and exceptional *sense of humor*.

The series' developed organically. How can wholistic health NOT include "True" humor?

See The SEQUEL to the lost exceptional *sense of humor* in The Domestic marine ® at corejokes.com. Also see: eatingforself.com.

When entering my teen years, my older brothers were no longer living at home and it seemed that now in addition to my subconscious "father-figure" mentality that I really was the "man of the house."

Had school work to complete and participated in sports and school activities such as the chess club . . . tried to repair a car that I bought and gave to my mother and rewired [Electrical] her entire house from top to bottom at age 14.

Interestingly, after making it to the finals in the chess tournament, my opponent and his supervising brother were collaborating together making sure of winning.

It was easy enough to recognize their tactics when they decided to write-down each move that was made and then hand the paper back and forth to each other. -- The older brother giving the next move to his younger brother while claiming to record the moves.

Instead of calling them on their motives, just played along, but decided to NOT even pay attention to the moves and present them with the most absurd move that could be made each Time-Toll that it was my turn. – Had to see the squirming? . . . They didn't start to relax until they saw that they had the game won. -- Of course, they could NOT have allowed me to win!

My teen years were progressing rapidly and what to do after graduation was MORE and MORE on my mind. . . . Had always known that college was the best option for me but how was it to be paid for was the question in my mind constantly.

Other parents were on welfare and welfare paid for their child's college but my mother had just become employed down at a steel mill and she had six children. -- Seemed to me like I was being punished for my mother working?

My decision was to go into the service after hearing about the Veteran's Educational Assistance Program (VEAP).

Please refer to the book entitled: The Domestic marine ®: Never Before and Never Again; There is ONLY One "Domestic marine" for MORE detailed explanations on military service truths, events and activities.

Thought this was a good place for one of my poems:

"God gave us boundaries so that we may make choices. When a person chooses to close their Heart, ♥ Mind, Ψ Soul, X "SELF" Δ then nothing gets in but evil knows no boundary. When one opens their Heart, ♥ Mind, Ψ Soul, X "SELF" Δ then they are filled with no room for evil. Choose to open your Heart, ♥ Mind, Ψ Soul, X "SELF" Δ and one will no longer have to choose to love; love will no longer be a choice?"

Chapter 2 – Online Encounter

Somewhere around 2014, since I was always messing around with computers, such as, building media center PCs (Audio/Video) for my immediate family and taking apart electronic equipment in general, it was mentioned to me that it would be quite profitable if I could come up with a WAY to mute a television commercial while at the same Time-Toll turning on the radio.

I didn't give this idea a whole lot of thought at the Time-Toll that it was mentioned to me because was aware that any manipulation of a broadcast signal had legal implications, after all, remember the 1980's attempts at this?

In 2014, however, had already decided to start writing my book. I'd decided that the Time-Toll had come to start focusing on my book writing after turning 50 years old. --My birthday is 12-30-1963.

Please see the book The Domestic marine ® for MORE details on why had chosen the age of 50 to begin a stronger focus on my book writing . . . (. . . Since the companion book has a romantic overtone, I'll give you one of the reasons now).

The first reason was because Mark Twain began his writing career at the age of 50. The other reasons are mentioned in the main book: The Domestic marine ® and the out-of-this-series Health, Diet & Recipe's Adventure Book Series main book: Eating for "SELF."

. . . Watched much television because had installed a couple cable-cards into my desktop media center PCs that built for me. --Liked to record basketball games to my hard drive and burn them to disc.

One day, must have been agitated about something because it seemed as though the television commercials would NOT end. . . . They must have had some extra man-made time slots to fill. --I couldn't take another commercial! . . . (The idea of muting and turning on the radio came to mind and it seemed like a great idea at this Time-Toll?).

Muting the television was NOT an issue but was so angry about the bombardment of commercials that wanted some recourse! . . . (Set my Heart, ♥ Mind, ψ Soul, X "SELF" Δ in analysis mode on this problem, once, and for all!).

Please see Book III of The Domestic marine ® Tandem Book Writing and "Equational" and Engendered Poetry Series with parallel writing: "The Silencer Project:" The Power of The "Night Sun" ☼ for the whole "Story," manuals and schematics on the Television Commercial Silencer Electrical Wall Outlet Receptacle Tap. --U.S. Patent NO. 10,249,996.

In January of 2017, now that my book writing was focused and had begun work on my Television Commercial Silencer Electrical Wall Outlet Receptacle Tap prototype and while watching the election results, decided to reopen Hassey Solutions, Old-Fashioned Service, Computer Business in Lehigh Acres, Florida.

(Please see the main book, Book III and Book III's companion book for MORE details on the reopening of Hassey Solutions computer business).

Never had any interest in social media until business pages became available so decided to create a social media business page to get the word out about my products and services but was NOT permitted to create the business page WITHOUT first creating a personal page.

Eager to get started, forgot to consider the reasons that never had any interest in social media in the first place; just moved forward with the creation of the personal page followed by Hassey Solutions business page, however, also decided to make productive use out of the "personal page" and use it to help "take my first 'True Life' back."

Wasn't long after creating the personal page that received my first friend request and it was from my Tomboy friend from childhood?

This online encounter with my Tomboy childhood friend was the last thing that I expected at this Time-Toll because she was already the focal point of my childhood in my book The Domestic marine ® as my childhood first love!

Side Note: Unlike in the Philippines, a Tomboy in the United States is NOT a homosexual?

After reading Sub Chapter 1 – Getting To The Heart ♥ of The Matter, Chapter 3 – Trophy Love, ♦ Sub Chapter 3 – The Angel One, MORE details are given about the Online Encounter in Chapter 4 – The Tomboy "Story."

It became necessary to continue this "Story," Chapter 2 – Online Encounter, in Chapter 4 – The Tomboy "Story" because this pair of books was written in Tandem with one another, ("Tandem Books,") while also, at Time-Tolls, engaging social media.

Therefore, the books became "LIVING BOOKS" and organization and restructuring was required throughout the manuscript writing and presentation process.

"Tandem Book" writing NOT only produced a literary original work and first of its kind literary construct in "LIVING BOOKS", but is the first success "Story" to merge the real and virtual worlds for the betterment in relationships for all and the promotion of positive social change.

The online encounter evolved WITHIN Chapter 4 – The Tomboy Story, coming-up, stay-tuned:

Sub Chapter 2 – Getting to The Heart ♥ of The Matter

2017 social media post: "Failed to mention, there will be a few things about relationships in my book as well."

"This has nothing to do with YOU directly, and I hope that you don't mind my sharing it, but some of my recent research and experiences have allowed me to draw certain conclusions about my own life and experiences while noticing others have been finding correlation? Sent this message to some and some seem to relate?"

"I'm trying to build interest for my book because marketing and advertising are so skewed and corrupt today:"

"It's MORE than $400.00 close to $500.00 for non provisional patent. That's what I need. Good for about 20 years and there are some maintenance costs after so many years? NOT many realize how difficult it is for someone in my situation to pull-off some of the things that I have! I'm NOT wealthy and never had any support, as a matter of truth, just the opposite! My book has much that has NOT yet been disclosed and I don't think anyone will fully understand until they read the series(s)! That's why been so aggressively trying to market early! It's hard to get the word out through normal channels. I wish things were different but I never compromised my principles for anything my entire first or now second "True Life" and I'm NOT about to start now! My own family did NOT even contribute a single dollar to my Kickstarter campaign and I'm NOT even sure if they would be willing to buy my book; they'd expect me to give it to them? All that I've been doing recently and really my whole first "True Life" has been for their benefit and others as well and a consequence to that just happened TO BE helping me in the end but people are so bitter in their own lives that when they see someone climbing the 'ladder,' they instinctively try to knock them down. Misery loves company!"

Sorry for any intrusion!

Here's a repeat of one of my poems: "God gave us boundaries so that we may make choices. When a person chooses to close their Heart, ♥ Mind, ψ Soul, X "SELF" Δ then nothing gets in but evil knows no boundary. When one opens their Heart, ♥ Mind, ψ Soul, X "SELF" Δ then they are filled with no room for evil. Choose to open your Heart, ♥ Mind, ψ Soul, X "SELF" Δ and one will no longer have to choose to love; love will no longer be a choice."

Today's my 54th birthday (December 30) but thought I'd do things a little differently and give everyone else a gift today . . . last Poem of 2017:

" . . . ..was told that I'm out of sync with society, but, how could this be, when God just sent me an angel in my Time-Toll of need? Therefore, must be in God's thoughts, and there's no place that I'd rather be, so I'm NOT out of sync with society; society's out of sync with me!"

Chapter 3 – Trophy Love ♦

It seemed that each encounter with my Tomboy friend, while growing up, was a challenge to gain her attentions, once she decided to start pulling away from me after our significant moment that was described in Chapter 1 – Early Childhood.

All the boys that she seemed to interact with treated her poorly WITHOUT respect while she appeared to be drawn to this type of attentions from those boys.

I was NOT comfortable seeing her treated that WAY, however, and began an even MORE exaggerated "Nice guy" approach to gaining her attentions and showed her even MORE respect than I already had.

Today, can see that I also started to hide my *sense of humor* from her in an attempt to show even MORE respect, pushing her even farther away with this approach.

My Tomboy friend became the source of my childhood depression by forcing me to suppress some passions, angers and even some humor so as NOT to lose my "Nice guy" approach, because I didn't want to be like the other boys.

There was, what I thought, the most lovely looking girl at school much MORE attractive than my Tomboy first love, but I always simply ignored her because my attentions were held on my first love.

However, since I was having no success at getting closer to my Tomboy friend, my attentions began to focus on the most lovely looking girl at school. [Took a long Time-Toll to realize that, subconsciously, this was a deliberate act to try to make my first love jealous]. –My first experience with "Trophy Love!" ♦ and my first loss of some personal confidence but realize today that I never gave the effort!

While focusing on this beautiful girl at school, in the hopes of gaining my Tomboy friend's attentions, absolutely did fall in love with her, but knew nothing of her! We never interacted with each other, to any significant degree, simply adored her appearance.

In later grades, as she got older, discovered that what a waist of my little efforts to love and care for someone that quite frankly was much too "'SELF'-less" and "'SELF'-less" motivated (See "Equational Poetry) ™ for me to ever experience any kind of lasting relationship with, because my giving nature required a MORE reciprocating girl, a person can only give so much WITHOUT receiving something! --Maybe this was why that I never gave my full efforts in the first place?

At this point, I started to accept the realization that there may NOT be a girl for me in my neighborhood or attending my school or grade at least. --My maturity level and "SELF"-imposed subconscious "father-figure" mentality seemed to keep me focused on the higher grades, however.

There was that one girl, the only girl, younger than I, that troubled me! She always drew my attention even away from my first love, so much so that avoided her, maybe subconsciously at Time-Tolls, that became MORE difficult with each encounter! She wasn't just lovely but adorable and the sweetest girl at the school and in the neighborhood! --I wanted her heart ♥ so badly but she seemed taboo ♠ to me! --It seemed almost like I was cheating on my first love!

I never attempted to steal her heart but she stole mine, ♥ WITHOUT even doing anything!

I would continuously lose the focus on her and as mentioned make efforts to avoid her because of the simplicity of attractiveness. --I Would have loved her friendship, as so desired, in my Tomboy first love, and she had the beauty contained and desired WITHIN my Trophy Love ♦ and she also had the most desirable heart, ♥ so filled with pure love ☼ + ☽ = * and genuine affections, that she seemed to be a necessity almost or at least a compliment to my giving nature!

In my efforts to understand where this taboo ♠ arose and bring it to words, recalled an encounter with this girl's father at their home on our street where we lived.

Her family lived two houses down from my childhood home for some Time-Toll before moving. This encounter has always been the most vivid of encounters with this girl's father but never knew why until the writing of my manuscripts.

Recalled her father cleaning bluegill fish caught down at the railroad tracks at the bottom of our street and he tossed the filets on an open fire in his back yard. . . . Down at the tracks we called the bridge, "black bridge," going over the river and their was a pond that we called, "Banana pond."

I'm NOT sure who caught the bluegill but this girl's father appeared to me to be a man of means. He was quite the handyman and seemed to be the type that took pride in everything that he did, had ingenuity, natural skills and high character. --He was everything that a young kid like me would want in a father. --I think this is where my conflict and taboo ♠ started while my

"SELF"-imposed subconscious "father-figure" mentality carried it forward and to an extreme?

Do remember, while listening to him speak and dropping some bluegill filets on the fire, glancing over and seeing his daughter and son, his wife also appeared, --quite the mature and responsible, loving and hardworking type. --Compassionate and steadfast came to mind, commanding respect!

I remember thinking that his daughter was already desirable enough and to have a father and be part of this wholesome family was something that I craved, but it would have been necessary to yield somewhat as I was just of a child's age, however, my personal "SELF-imposed subconscious "father-figure" mentality and assumed responsibilities to my own family could NOT allow for that! –Looking back now, I'm NOT sure, if I ever did have a childhood and unfortunately by choosing NOT to yield to her father, was also choosing NOT to yield to my own desires or even the chance of a relationship with his daughter or him or his family.

With that, ♠ taboo, I could NOT risk hurting her, if I were the type of person that contemplates regrets, this, and NOT taking the Time-Toll to "smell the flowers" thorough-out my first "True Life," that my subconscious "father-figure" mentality prevented me from doing most of the Time-Tolls, would be my ONLY regrets, but regrets are a form of "SELF" pity ♣ so I don't bother contemplating them but prefer to avoid them, by starting a new, with a gentler approach to my "SELF," because I've been as gentle to the world as possible. --It's Time-Toll to yield to some desires!

If I were to define his daughter today, the only definition that could possibly make any kind of sense to me would be "The Angel One!" She was a girl worth dedicating a book too, and my entire life, so I thought!

In summary, my Tomboy friend forced me to suppress some *passions* and *anger* and *humor* by turning them into depression, to be someone other than my "SELF." --In The Domestic marine, ® discuss when, NOT just some humor, but my *sense of humor* was suppressed and also felt discarded-- . . . my attempts at *Trophy Love* ♦ took some of my personal confidence away and then The Angel One stole my heart ♥ while at the Time-Toll of some of these writings, now that I have taken my first "True Life" back, thought that it was time to return the favor, and steal hers', because that was always my strongest desire!

Sub Chapter 3 – The Angel One

I've never had any support from anyone or any entity my whole first "True Life" and I would have been okay with that, but people set out to intentionally hurt me my whole first "True Life," and it wasn't just women but men too!

R and "Others" were envious of me because I had NOTHING, but was still secure in my "SELF!" They could NOT stand it!

Je's brother that I also wrestled with had D fired! This is when I stopped putting on a show for everyone in the wrestling matches, but in the practice room over at the junior high, no one could beat me in a match!

Je's liked me and R knew that! Am I making sense to you?

Before people "discard" you, they like to hurt you first!" It's NOT just women that do this but men too!

This is why It has been simpler for me to be alone. I'm just exhausted from being hurt!

Don't let this bother you J, I'm better right now at this point in my first "True Life" than I have ever been, both physically and mentally and when I've been at my worst point, I made it through!

SMILE ... or else! lol

P.S. Listen to that song! "Sometime [tolls] when we touch" by Dan Hill (The original by Dan Hill. He's from Canada). There have been others that sang and remade his song. They suck!

J, I also liked your father! Out of an extreme respect for him the taboo ♠ was even stronger!

--Note to "SELF:" Had my own responsibilities that prevented me from seeking my own desires. --

I liked D too! Kinda looked after him when in the ball field. He was a good kid! Your whole family was refreshing because most of the "families" on our street were NOT as wholesome as yours!

I'm going to back off, J, cause I don't want to scare you but remember that I am writing a couple of books and my intention was always to be brutally honest because this is what is wrong with society. . . . I'm NOT even joking when I say that I'm the only honest person that I know! It's scary J! Everyone lies! It's the culture! It's built-in and expected! What the hell? lol

. . . I'll tell ya, can see you as clearly as if it happened yesterday, pulling out a chair in the high school cafeteria looking a bit frazzled sitting down next to Rick as if you needed his support and me just wondering what in the hell, of all the guys that she could have, why him? . . . I wanted to be the one to comfort you because I knew that Rick was NOT capable of it!

Sorry! Had to get that off of my chest! Just wanted to let you know that you HAVE TO buy my books now cause in the companion book, you are now Sub Chapter 3 – The Angel One. --The sub chapters are MORE meaningful to me, by the way!

I've been writing the books in tandem lately as inspiration strikes!

Sorry again, J! I had no intention of sending this E-mail but in continuing my writing of Sub Chapter 3, learned something about my "SELF" for the first Time-Toll in my first "True Life!" (I credit you for that!)!

When I first mentioned to you that I was planning on dedicating the companion book to you, you said, but "I didn't do anything."

That's one of the things that I loved about you! You're clueless!

Just being you was help enough! Thanks!

Well, guess that my memory is NOT perfect but it always comes back if I think hard enough!

It was E that had D fired. D was the only one that ever tried to help me, in junior high or high school. He got the school to pay for two wrestling camps that I went to.

That's why E pissed me off and it did have a little to do with the truth that his sister Char liked me.

I think you're talking about Je? Wasn't it Je that Rick cheated on you with? I believe that she liked me too but NOT positive? E's sister Char definitely did! -- They were both cheerleaders.

Either one, for R to leave you for, still proves that he was an idiot! You were adorable in high school and you were probably the sweetest girl that I remember but to be perfectly honest with you, I was kinda stupid in some WAYs back then?

I was always mature for my age and most, if NOT all, the guys that I spent time around were older than I. I felt out of place with most in my own grade and I was "SELF" conscious about asking a younger girl out.

How clearly silly a notion that was I see now but back then there was something taboo ♠ about dating younger grades. R was a year older than I was and he liked to go after the younger girls because he thought that they were MORE easily taken advantage of. Do I have it right now?

Chapter 4 – The Tomboy Story

Side Note: Unlike in the Philippines, a Tomboy in the United States is NOT a homosexual?

After receiving my childhood first love's "Friend" request and since she was already in my book, my first thought was that I was right all along and that she must still have some feelings toward me; I was elated!

Shortly, grew saddened though when several days had past and she still had NOT responded to my reply to her request. -- I was NOT sure how to proceed with my work from here?

Finally, after several days she responded, and typically, she offered little of her "SELF" but had many questions. . . . -- My nature is to spill my guts while other men will say that's the last thing that one wants to do with a woman!

Plus, again, once a woman knows that a man is interested in her, so it begins, the ritualistic games or, since the man is no longer a challenge, the woman suddenly departs!

I had no Time-Toll for childish games as I had several projects running in parallel and was determined to "take back my first 'True Life!'" However, I loved this girl, like no other! -- I had to see what her intentions were, but, from the beginning, . . . had to "draw a line in the sand," something that I had never done with any woman in the past and would never have done with this woman at any other point in my first "True Life," but then!

The MORE that I spilled my guts, the MORE unintelligible her responses.

Therefore, I made my feelings absolutely clear to her and she stated, "I'll never feel that way about YOU." -- It hurt! -- Remember, had NOT seen or heard from her in over 30 years since high school and it really hurt! --That was new for me!

At least I knew what I needed to know so that I could get on with my projects and "taking back my first 'True Life!'" -- I did have to work for her friendship that she stated was all that we could ever have together.

I was okay with that but for some reason was compelled to tell her my deepest thoughts and feelings for her as a child?

She confessed that "no one has ever talked to me like that before!"

However, as impressed as she seemed to be with me, she maintained that we could never be MORE than friends. I conceded and said, "I'll always be grateful that I had the opportunity to tell YOU how I felt about YOU" and was absolutely planning on leaving it at that and getting on with my projects! . . . Wham! She drew me back into her unintelligible ritualistic games again.

She, prior to this point, was giving me advice on what to watch out for in a woman and she was spot-on in her details but after I shared my true feelings toward her, she began doing the things that she had just warned me to watch out for from a woman and she was NOT even aware of what she was doing.

It was scary, it was frightening, but it was comical too!

She had me so mixed up and confused that I had no clue what to believe from her anymore.

Suddenly, my crowdfunding efforts started to be realized and my online "Friends" began to grow exponentially right before her eyes and my Kickstarter Project began receiving attention and my childhood first love that just told me that she would never feel the same way about me as I did about her and that we could ONLY ever be friends, called me sweetie and offered to fly down and have dinner together.

. . . There was a deadline on my NON provisional Patent and did NOT have Time-Toll to sort-out what was going on in her head. I needed to see her to be able to determine her true feelings and intentions toward me! If it were any other woman, It would NOT have been necessary to go to such an extent but as I said, I loved this girl like no other!

I decided to drive up to Pennsylvania to see her and she agreed that once I arrived she would buy me dinner at a Chinese restaurant near her home and also arrange a get-together with other high school classmates of mine.

Her and I were E-mailing, texting and even spoke on the phone together. She also gave me her sister's mobile number to text and her daughter's E-mail address so that I could sign all of them up, to share my vacation points.

Unfortunately or fortuantely for me, as I was planning my trip up to Pennsylvania and flight into the Pittsburgh airport, one of her old high school boyfriends came out of NO where and offered me a ride from the Pittsburgh airport, but also fortunately for me, that is, while she remained unaware that I remembered her old boyfriends from high school, and recognized what was transpiring online, hence, my Tomboy first love from childhood found one of her old high school boyfriend via my efforts to see her while I was trying to determine her true feelings and intentions toward me, and, once again, it hurt!

She was able to find one of her high school boyfriends and hurt me at the sameTime-Toll because of my efforts, a win win! . . . I cried for several days, had never done that before but soon took solace in the truth that I was the one to bring her happiness. -- I hold onto that sentiment to this Time-Toll and it gave me a warm feeling inside.

The night prior to my Tomboy friend from childhood finding one of her high school boyfriends, my dreams were asking me if I wanted to release something of hers that I was holding onto all of those years! I would have never let go of whatever it was that I was holding onto of hers any other Time-Toll in my first "True Life" but this was my best opportunity to "take back my first 'True' Life'" and my Tomboy first love had just prior told me that "YOU have to start letting people go!"

Therefore, when my dreams that night asked me if I wanted to let go of whatever it was that I was holding onto of hers, I said yes, since that was what my Tomboy childhood first love wanted! . . .

Something of hers left me that "Night Star" * night!

I still wanted to see her and make sure that she was alright.

By chance, and through my computer skills, I stumbled upon yet MORE plot and intentions discovering a distributed chat system directing each of my messages to my Tomboy friend to multiple destinations. – They teamed-up on me and were playing me.

Another of my childhood friends that liked me growing-up was receiving my messages along with my Tomboy friend and a gay guy.

The gay guy was used to filter and interpret the male ego while my Tomboy friend was trying to drive me into the arms of another woman that truly liked me of a child's age.

I never let on that I knew what they were up to but this knowledge served me well in the days to come!

-- While I was driving to Pennsylvania to see her, I pulled over and dosed-off at a rest stop and a dream told me to take a different route then I had originally planned to take; the new route took me into Ohio instead of Pennsylvania and the last text message from my Tomboy childhood first love instructed me to go to my mother's house in Ohio and text her from there. I did exactly as she requested but no one wanted to get-together with me and my childhood Tomboy first love's final public online post to me accused me of stocking.

After a quite painful, something else that I had never experienced to that extent, short visit at my mother's house in Ohio and after the 2017 total eclipse of the sun ☼ + ☽ = * that Monday, drove back to Florida and again, it hurt!

My Tomboy friend connected me with a old male childhood classmate of ours that was currently working in Tampa, Florida and I drove several hours to meet-up with him.

This is where the previous knowledge of plot and intentions unfolded.

This old friend had a pressure-washing business and was living in a trailer on land owned by one of his friends.

He wanted me to finance a camper and sign a rent-to-own agreement to place the camper on a portion of this same land. -- My Tomboy friend mentioned she wanted to sell her camper?

Prior to my meet-up with this guy I had connected my oldest brother with him because my oldest brother and three of his sons had their own pressure-washing business in Bonita Springs/Naples, Florida.

I had forgotten that I connected my brother with this guy but when asking him what him and my brother talked about on the phone my eyes were fully open. My brother all WAYs liked my Tomboy friend's oldest sister?

I read the rental agreement that was offered on the camper and found a back-end loan. I was aware of back-end loans from my student loan days.

The friend in Tampa, remember, grew-up in Ohio like me where the back-end student loan was invented. I exposed the back-end student loan years before this online encounter. The camper would never have been paid-off with such a loan and would create a perpetual debt as the government did with student loans and the government even made the next of kin responsible for paying off these student loans even after the responsible party was dead. Evil at its best!

Finally, it turns out that I am grateful to my childhood first love, NOT ONLY for providing me the opportunity to tell her how I truly felt about her, but also the opportunity to release what it was of hers that I was holding onto all of those years. Her spell was returned to her to recast upon her old boyfriend, while I was freed to start a new journey and adventure! I now know what it was that I released of hers that "Night Star" * night, and exactly what I gained; my passion, now available for MY "True Love." *♥ΨΧΔ

After months of recovery, and while continuing work on my projects, shortly, thereafter, received another friend request from another childhood love of mine. . . . What are the odds?

-- ONLY, this love was deeper, inside, somewhere? --Some MORE sorting to do, Time-Toll to resolve, the

"Trophy Love!" ◆

Besides Chapter 3 of this book above, The "Trophy Love" ♦ chapter can be found expounded upon in the main book, The Domestic marine: ® Never before and Never again; There is ONLY one "Domestic marine"

--Yes, it's Time-Toll to move on to a MORE structured second "True Life." Stay tuned!

Sub Chapter 4 – My Burnt Store Friend

Someone once told me that the bible says that one is supposed to protect their heart ♥ above all else?

The guy that told me this even has a tattoo of the bible verse on his chest, due to his recent (At the Time-Toll of this manuscript writing) hard luck first "True Life" lessons and he believed that this bible verse meant that one is supposed to keep their heart ♥ closed and choose when to open it?

There is a misconception here.

My first "True Life" lessons have taught me that one is always suppose to keep their heart ♥ open! The WAY to protect one's heart ♥ is to keep one's heart ♥ true and pure! *

One must let everything into their heart ♥ and one's Heart, ♥ Mind, ψ Soul, X "SELF" Δ will sort it out!

I've been told that my approach to "True Life" has always been one of following my heart ♥ with God at my back!

This is how I conduct my "True Life!"

If a person's heart ♥ contains ONLY true *♥ and pure ☼ + ꜟ love, then, if one follows their heart, ♥ God will be at their back to help sort out and someTime-Tolls even determine the consequences!

. . .

. . .

I had posted in 2024 that there would be MORE of Goose WITHIN The Domestic marine? ® – The Vietnam Veteran biker gang leader that I grew-up to admire.

The Vietnam Biker gangs on the Streets of what was once America, were groups of men that were demanding respect that they never received. Their facades were a loyalty to their gender, which would NEVER be NEUTRAL!

Vietnam Veterans were spit upon when returning to their homes, just as Selective Service orchestrated.

The Cold War NEVER ended, but rather, evolved into The Societal. --The "stress" WITHIN everyone's make-believe life today is orchestrated by the psyops of the day.

Just as NO one could speak to a Vietnam Veteran, unless they "were there," so too, NO one knows what it truly means to "swallow your pride, but shed a tear;" unless YOU were there?

With that, the same applies to "True Love."

"True Love" is what made Goose different. His leadership was NOT a facade, like the others, while respect, NEVER demanded; ALWAYS earned.

The point in mentioning Goose here in addition to writing of him WITHIN The Domestic marine ® is that Goose was NOTHING like "My Burnt Store 'Friend,'" who tuned-out, like my of a child's age Tomboy "friend,"

Thu Angel One and all those I grew-up with, and graduated from high school with, were NOT truly my friends either, while my wrestling coach, the Italian, X Marine was as immoral and unethical as an inhuman being could be, wonder who permitted him to teach in the school system, while I was blacklisted?

So called financial institutions, instruments as well as today's wealth management concepts are NOTHING like their original counterparts. The mere conceptualization of these systems guarantee that an upper class never need work again for they live off of those beneath.

A traditional "Bank" of yesteryear's does NOT exist today.

Alexander Hamilton was a criminal, an Aristocrat that kissed his king's ass. Alexander Hamilton made Thomas Jefferson the first president of corporate America terminating George Washington's efforts at creating a constitutionally based, of, by, and for the people "True" government.

Alexander Hamilton was the first U.S. Secretary of the treasury and founder of the world bank which was the end of "True" capitalism and country, for wealth, city, money economy and perpetual war and the new slavery.

The American Civil War was the fight for "True" capitalism that the Vietnam War was claimed fought over. "True" capitalism ended with the conceptualization of the world bank by Alexander Hamilton.

Trump spoke of returning to the gold standard during his first term in Washington D.C. while now in a historic election he joins filthy rich childish Elon Musk on an idea to eliminate the U.S. Treasury department for block-chain. -- Financial slavery.

Trump's association with Musk is clear evidence that once one enters Washington D.C. they become corrupt. Don't trust a single person in D.C. and start thinking about declared war, and I'm NOT talking about governments, but rather, the people against the ruling criminals through the use of the Federal Constitution as did Robert E. Lee.

Chapter 5 – Prior to Provisional Patent

Before delving WITHIN chapter 5 here's a lead-in to express my feelings on science and/or genetics:

In April 2024, I bought some watermelon seeds as I've done so many Time-Tolls since of a child's age, but MORE often than NOT, I simply got my watermelon seeds from a watermelon?

For the first Time-Toll in 50 years I bought a pack of watermelon seeds from a grocery store in the Philippines that were NOT black, but coated with a purple sticky substance of science.

Logic said the purple coating was a chemical fertilizer formulated to encourage sprouting.

Seed packaging companies need any edge that they can get and also need to sell outdated merchandise but seeds are NOT products or commodities, but "True Life" TO BE?

The purple chemicals give the seeds the best chance to sprout MOST likely, but the worst chance to grow MORE likely.

These purple seeds did sprout, but soon after died, while some black watermelon seeds that someone tossed in the garden from a watermelon at one of our cook-outs weeks after the planting and dying of the purple watermelon seeds are flourishing today WITHOUT any fertilizer or water, just rain.

-- Which is less than any other April and May in the Philippines because the U.S. troops are here so science put a hold on El Niño tampering, cloud dissipation in LA and weather event manipulation until they take-over Beijing?

NOT ONLY is it foolish to trust science but any company or government today.

The new Japanese human baby incubation machines will have addons such as genetic modification APPs, and shopping cart systems to place an order for the characteristics of the commodity of your choice? They'll be homeless lining-up to donate sperm and eggs to the donor banks for cash while 3D printer like baby incubators fill warehouses like cloud servers ready to process custom orders for women that rather NOT get fat. MORE evil entering Satan's digital world!

eatingforself.com.

Recall it was somewhere around 2014 that my oldest brother mentioned that if I could come-up with a WAY to mute the TV while turning on the radio, I'd make a lot of money?

My brother was money hungry like my mother. I blamed commercialization for their problem.

The ironic part is that they didn't want to watch the commercials just shop. Most people don't care what they buy they just want to shop and watching the commercials upsets them because they don't have the money to go to the mall.

I all WAYS disliked money, Walmart, malls, oil companies, CORPORATISM, COMMUNISM, The Bastard and Bitch but commercials were Satan's best work and the worst.

This chapter is continued WITHIN the The Silencer Project's, Book III, companion book, The Poker Game Algorithm: Put One's "SELF" on the Table...

What today is termed the Privileged-class was termed the Nobility during the "First-Renaissance?"

The Privileged-class all WAYs speak of COMPLIANCE, but NEVER PRINCIPLE. Why is that, YOU think?

The Privileged-class, like the Nobility, will KISS any master's ass for free TO BE the petty-ass-class in reality, YOU SEE?

With that, a child domain is NOT the same as glue records by name.

Furthermore, like DNSSEC, the petty-ass-class implementation vary to COMPLIANCE rather than use STANDARDS; what's best for them rather than their "subjects," so they can sit on their petty-asses for a fake-lifetime?

What one thinks they understand, they don't?

Anyone that wants to truly understand the NUANCES of child domains and glue records, pick-up a companion book?

Chapter 6 – Prior to NON Provisional Patent

On the drive up to Ohio I also spoke to one of my sisters on the phone and through our conversation I sensed the emotional abuse that was waiting for me from my family, NOT just my old "friends."

While in Ohio waiting on the text message promised by my Tomboy "friend," My sisters refused to respond to my messages and phone calls, my mother said she didn't love me anymore, my brother put me through hell.

The "friends" from high school that I reached out to either did NOT answer or made a joke out of me.

The childhood and high school "friend" that did the Kickstarter video for me would NOT see me so I wired the money for the video to him?

The high school "friend" that was staying in Tampa called me, I'm sure to play with me some MORE.

I met with one "friend" from high school at a bar and bought him and his wife drinks all night but they were seeing if it was really me after all the years and ONLY interested in what I could do for them?

There were ONLY two other points in my first "True Life" that were worse than the experience of this trip.

I learned what I needed to know and when I returned to Florida I realized that it was my oldest brother that sabotaged my efforts to start a relationship with my Tomboy friend because he spoke with the high school "friend" of mine staying in Tampa. Both my brother and the guy in Tampa had their own pressure washing businesses so I connected them to one another to possibly help each other in business? My brother, who also liked the older sister of my Tomboy "friend," once again set me up for failure and involved the entire family and "friends." -- who needs enemies?

When I got back to Florida, I began working on the NON provisional patent? A provisional utility patent expires 12 months after issue and one must either convert it to a NON provisional or file a new NON provisional? I decided to file a new NON provisional patent after filing the provisional utility patent and I claimed priority on the provisional?

Claiming priority on the provisional patent in my view gave it value before it expired by allowing me to hold onto the January 2017 filing date as the date of first invention, which turned out TO BE a wise decision because some guy tried to claim my invention almost word for word his own but he didn't realize that I had filed a provisional and claimed priority, thus, his dates were off, so his theft of my work was for NOT?

It was December 2017 when I finally finished-up the NON provisional utility patent.\

Additionally, successfully opened and certified my own U.S. patent office account for filing purposes.

I filed the NON provisional and received my filing receipt.

It was after the 12 month mark when I heard from the patent office by letter.

The letter stated that the claims were unacceptable because they were in narrative form instead of a standard form? The examiner ONLY gave me 30 days, but from date of letter, to correct and resubmit just the claims, which gave me less than two weeks.

I did NOT find this reasonable or possible as I was working through the regular mail?

He was forcing me to get an attorney.

I didn't know how to go about getting an attorney because I had discovered when notified that I was eligible for student loan reimbursement a couple years prior, but was refused the same, that LEE COUNTY, FLORIDA was the ONLY county in Florida with a private attorney referral service?

The corruption in LEE COUNTY, Florida blocked me from anything and everything I had ever attempted as a human being for 30 + years.

The attorney that I had to get to fight for the student loan reimbursement a couple years earlier before the patent took half, $5000.00.

-- I also hit Hyundai with the Federal Lemon Law at this Time-Toll and remember the tow truck driver in the main book that I made come to the cabin in the wildlife preserve and load the 2016 Food Escape, sold to me as a brand new 2017 after Ford turned back the mileage, that I added to my business and personal bankruptcy? --

Additionally, used this attorney, to get a new air conditioner, at the apartment complex that I lived for 8 years, as the ONLY one to never miss a rent payment, after going MORE than a month WITHOUT AC, when it is state law that a landlord must provide air conditioning?

After paying him and getting the new air conditioner, the apartment complex new owner forced me out and blacklisted me so moving forward I needed a private owner landlord. I could NOT rent from any MORE managed communities because this new owner bought them all in LEE county?

Thank God for hurricanes and The Domestic marine. ®

I would NOT utilize the attorney referral service or online search engines as they too are all corrupt, especially in LEE COUNTY, FLORIDA so I used the old-school phone book yellow pages to prime my search and stay anonymous?

The first patent attorney that I called, after explaining my filing of the provisional and then the NON provisional while choosing to claim priority of the provisional instead of converting it, interrupted me and said that, he didn't believe that I did all that because he had been doing patents for 30 years and that they were hard for him?

As the conversation continued, I recognized that he was NOT up to date on his knowledge of procedure of the patent office as I had just filed a provisional and NON provisional and was utilizing current research.

Like any job or carrier today, one must stay up to date on the changes and innovations, however, once an attorney of privilege buys his WAY into the "profession," they need NOT know anything as they are assured that their clients need them, just as government mandates? Therefore, those in the highest places are the MOST incompetent.

I told him that I was going to check prices and would get back to him?

Licked my thumb and turned the yellow page, after page, after page.

Called another number but he said that he NO longer did patents but knew a dependable guy in NAPLES, FLORIDA, collier county. That appealed to me because LEE COUNTY and me were NOTHING if NOT enemies?

NAPLES was 30 minutes south, county to county, but I was coming from the wildlife preserve, which was Punta Gorda, until Cape Coral annexed it?

MORE like an hour drive for me to this NAPLES, FLORIDA patent attorney in Collier county?

All this attorney wanted TO BE assured of was if I had a computer repair business in LEE county as I claimed because he knew that if that were the case then I was part of the privileged class and that I was someone that he was permitted to help because CORPORATISM's philosophy of economics is wrapped around the concept of waist, that is, master-slave, that is, the new financial slavery and MANDATES?

The attorney and his partner that did the notations and formality work, and I, discussed the details of the provisional and NON provisional utility patents, that I had all ready completed and filed, I also informed them that the NON provisional had all ready expired.

I explained my concern with the man-made time limit on submitting the needed format adjustment on the claims.

The attorney said, "as you know, the claims are the most important part of a patent."

To submit what you need, will cost you $2,500.00. Since you have a computer repair business, I'm guessing that won't be a problem?

Bit my tongue, but said, I'll need a little Time-Toll?

The patent was done and the patent office said it was a format issue, formality?

The attorney, in essence, was receiving $2,500.00 to have his boy take notes, secretary put my words in a template and click submit.

I conducted the necessary transaction with his secretary over the phone the following week.

It was a week or two later when I received an E-mail of the examiner's decision and then a phone call from the attorney saying, he got the patent.

After reviewing the newly submitted claims, including those claims the examiner accepted and which were rejected, I told the attorney during the phone call that "WE" can do better! He didn't like that, but it was also exactly what he wanted to hear. He just wanted me to soften my approach with him. I was all ready at my wits end with greedy idiots. I told him to followup with a demand for all the claims. He said that's a continuation. I said to continue demanding all of my claims.

While the attorney was preparing to file his continuation of the NON provisional patent, I received a letter from the Marine Corp Trademark Communication Office. -- I also applied for a trademark on The Domestic marine in parallel with the patents. -- My intention, since of a child's age, was to write a single book, while the title idea of The Domestic marine came about in the early 1990s, the Trademark idea came in 2017.

The letter stated that the Marine Corp Trademark Communication Office had over 200 trademarks with the word Marine in them and that their office was going to monitor my progress, that was 2018.

The Domestic marine mark was NOT registered yet at this Time-Toll.

All trademarks enter a dispute phase 30 days before registration WITHIN the National Gazette.

On the 30th day, last day before registration and publication of The Domestic marine, the Marine Corp Trademark Communication Office, WITHOUT prior discovery, disputed my federal trademark application of a book title trademark of The Domestic marine. -- The mark went into legal process.

As I was all ready utilizing an Intellectual Properties law firm for the NON provisional patent claims, I consulted the same on the filing of a response to the trademark office on The Domestic marine's behalf?

The attorney demanded an evergreen retainer of $10,000.00.

As this is Book II, **The Furthest and Nearest Night Stars: The Birth of The Night Star * 1st edition,** one can continue reading about the disputed book title trademark of The Domestic marine ® and unprecedented two following formal protests by the Marine Corps Trademark Communication Office leading to The Black Hill's Time Capsule Trip, beginning in Florida, while ending after returning to Dallas, Texas from Indonesia with a bell clock, in Book I, the main book in The Domestic marine ® Tandem Book Writing and "Equational" and Engendered Poetry Series with parallel writing, entitled: The Domestic marine: ® Never Before and Never Again; There is ONLY one "Domestic marine."

I never trusted this attorney and like during the custody battle for my two daughters in LEE COUNTY, Florida beginning back in 1989 when the divorce attorney immediately put a lean on the house I had built in Cape Coral, Florida with a VA loan upon giving him a $2,500.00 retainer for any future owed monies, I got rid of him. "True Life" is too short to have these types WITHIN.

I began building Intellectual Property to turn the tables on the Marine Corp Trademark Communication Office, starting with application of an International patent on The Television Commercial Silencer

Electrical Wall Outlet Receptacle Tap, U.S. Patent NO 10,249,996, but hired a different law firm to file it.

A couple E-mails with the original claim's adjusting attorney follow:

This chapter is continued WITHIN the main book in The Domestic marine ® Tandem Book Writing and "Equational" and Engendered Poetry Series with parallel writing, entitled: The Domestic marine: ® Never Before and Never Again; There is ONLY one "Domestic marine."…

Ed:

The rejection by the examiner appears to be due to prior art of a remote controlled standard power strip or multi outlet standard AC outlet extension? The patent was requesting protection on a remote controlled standard AC extension outlet for general use for electronic devices, like a TV, for normal operation of the electronic device.

Beyond powering on and off, there was no concept of any other usage mentioned.

Moreover, the attached power outlet module that I designed is what is being objected to by the examiner based on the prior art of a remote controlled standard power outlet extension for on/off of household appliances.

However, my outlet's distinctive configurations provide a specific purpose and circuit design that the prior art can NOT achieve even if a concept was included WITHIN the prior art but wasn't?

My circuit designs are also low voltage and NOT meant for use as standard AC wall outlet receptacles but specifically for low voltage audio systems and devices and are user configurable?

In addition, my outlet configurations utilize a WiFi remote controlled power unit as well and these WiFi modules are sold for just such purpose of my intent, as are generic remote control power modules for electronic designs of one's own conception.

The Silencer is NOT employing or conceiving or implementing a prior manufactured remote control power strip for standard AC power extension to standard electronic devices for normal operation, but rather a distinctive and specific design and purpose that are configurable and upgradable.

See attached Silencer Outlet Configuration Module design. Plus, this is my ONLY Module that is being objected to NOT the one's that follow.

I have another point to be made that will also overcome the examiner's rejections that I will send shortly. I wanted to send my points separately so as NOT to confuse the distinctions?

Ed:

In the attached TV Configuration Module of my design, there is a clear distinction of "The Remote Controlled External Television Audio System Outlet." (A Specific and Distinctive purpose) However, no "OUTLET" truly exists!

The diagram merely symbolically depicts the power source in diagram method but all electronics and circuitry are contained WITHIN the Silencer and the power is taped from a secondary source after being received from the WiFi module or Remote control Power Module but NOT from a standard electrical power outlet of any kind and again the power being utilized is of a low voltage nature that a standard power outlet can NOT provide, NOR the design or configurations or upgradability?

One has to be able to plug in their designed device, all electronic component's require power to operate? One cannot patent electricity itself because it is NOT an invention but a discovery!

In addition, I can supply power or cut the power for the Television Audio System WITHIN this TV Module or the Radio internal Module or MP3 Player internal Module or Optical Audio Module or any other device's Audio Module all fully contained WITHIN the Silencer any where that I choose to and can also disrupt the audio signal itself rather than the power source such as in the 3.5mm Audio/Headphone Ports to accomplish the same end result?

These are just some distinctions that are apparent but I have further as well as the proprietary audio and/or power ports and cabling that would entirely circumvent any rejection's by the examiner?

Ed:

There's a saying, "**Shoot for the furthest star ☼ and the nearest star ➍ is easier to grasp**!" Actually, Ed, I've done so much creative writing and developed such a personal poetic writing style that I'm NOT sure if that's an old Chinese proverb or if I just made it up now? LOL

Anyway, I did NOT thoroughly study the prior art because quite frankly it did NOT impress me. I've been out-pacing the electronics's industry since the Internet began. I had no choice in the matter while many people expressed to me that in the years to come that I would NOT be able to keep-up with the industry paces. However, that has NOT been the case in the slightest. I never moved on with my studies of any subject during my education until I was satisfied that I had a solid grasp of the subject matter. I have a rock solid foundation to the industry and built every layer a top of said foundation as the layers presented themselves and now I added some of my own layers finally because all of my layers in my past were simply stolen from me!

Based on the prior art that YOU submitted to me for my review, I do NOT see anything that would preclude our **grasping that furthest star** ☼ and all the rest along the way!

For the same reason that I presented to YOU above for why many believed that I would be out-paced by the industry, it appears to me that others have NOT attempted to keep pace and simply conceded to the industry. I am so grateful to YOU, Ed, in many ways and one of those ways is that YOU just confirmed with the information from the Patent Office that YOU recently sent to me that this is in deed the case!

People have simply lost hope and are buying into this fallacy that the American Dream no longer exists. YOU have just added much "Human Intelligence" to some chapters in my book, thank YOU!

All this prior art that YOU have sent to me is mechanical in nature and serves their own distinctions and much of it has nothing to do with the electronics's industry but other industries while the ONLY prior art that was sent to me that warranted a closer study is for an entirely different purpose and of a general appeal, NOT specific like mine and bluntly there should be no way that the examiner can disagree with our distinctions in our amended claims. In truth, the specific prior art that I am referring to that is a general apparatus could be purchased along side my Silencer after manufacturing as a supporting device but incorporating additional outlet's WITHIN my device shall be allowed for this reason and it is a quite valid reason, that is, standard wall outlet power receptacles are freely used and the specific distinction in my invention that I am referring to is that besides standard freely used power outlet receptacles, my power outlet receptacles are NOT of a general type but rather the distinction is that they are designed specifically for audio devices of a low voltage type and for specialized purposes.

The prior art mechanism can NOT be interchanged with my invention's distinction and perform the same function WITHOUT serious issues to consider, WITHIN my circuit designs.

Chapters and Sub Chapters 7, 8, 9 – The Poker Game Algorithm of mine

I was the ONLY one that graduated from then Edison Community College in 1992 in Fort Myers, Florida with an "analysis" added to their programming degree, because of my skills to diagnose problems along with my leadership qualities as well as abilities to help others along the WAY.

My final project was designing an electronic poker card game.

The Instructor of the Turbo PASCAL programming course, who was also my academic advisor, and assigned by Edison Community College TO BE 100% responsible for my gainful employment, assigned the graduation projects.

This Turbo PASCAL course that was required for graduation was my second time around because this same Instructor failed me the first time I took the course.

The previous Turbo PASCAL course that I had failed the previous quarter was the first programming course that I had ever failed WITHIN the 5 years that I attended then Edison Community College in Fort Myers, Florida, beginning at the Collier County Branch in Naples, Florida, and, while looking back, I see now that the failure was due to my proficiency of the language, while helping every other student along my programming journey.

My Veterans Administration Vocational Rehabilitation counselor at the Federal Building in Miami, Florida told me to "never let Edison Community College forget that they are responsible for finding YOU a job."

The challenge that I found while coding an electronic poker game in Turbo PASCAL, besides the graphics, at the time, was in making sure that a card from the deck of 52 could NOT be dealt twice, in time.

My solution was in building an array(52) of a deck of 52 (cells) cards, but with the twist of an iterated loop to include a recursive trip through the array(52) with every dealt card from the initial deck and remove it from the array(52-1) deck with every dealt card thereafter to expect.

The Poker Game Algorithm became poetic.

Everyone in the computer lab followed my progress on the poker game project, and after assigning ASCI characters to each card, ♥♣♦♠ everyone said that if I scanned in face cards that my electronic poker game was marketable?

I compiled my Turbo PASCAL source code into an executable (.exe) before turning the completed program and project into the Instructor for a final grade.

The Instructor insisted that I give him the source code, which became a condition of passing the course, therefore, graduating, after I initially refused to do so?

His plans were to open his own software design company?

In 1992, there were NO other options for continuing one's education in Southwest Florida   so my plans were to move to Tampa, Florida and attend the University of South Florida but my programming degree was an AS, Associates in Science degree and my understanding was that an AA degree, Associate of Arts degree was required to enter a university, YOU see?

My graduating programming Instructor and academic advisor that most said was homosexual at then Edison Community College told me that he could get me into the University of South Florida in Tampa, Florida with my AS degree because of my leadership qualities?

I was also working as a cashier at Circle K convenience store at night and the manager said that I could transfer to a Circle K in Tampa?

Some Time-Toll after handing the Instructor the source code for the final graduation project and finalizing my departure from Circle K in Fort Myers, I received my AS degree in the mail as I did NOT attend the graduation ceremony.

I began planning my move to Tampa, to transfer to a Circle K and enroll for classes for the next quarter at the University of South Florida.

My brother and his girlfriend decided to move with me. My brother said he always wanted to live in Tampa and his girlfriend's father lived there, who my brother claimed they got along better with than her mother?

I loaded a U-haul with all of my belongings and attached my car in tow, while I, with my oldest brother and his girlfriend, drove to Tampa in the U-haul together.

At this point I had already secured the apartment at a complex with first, last and security deposit ($1500) in all.

Once we arrived at the apartment complex and furnished the apartment with my belongings, I headed by my "SELF" to Circle K. After arriving, the manager said that "we're NOT hiring at this time?"

Angrily, I drove to the University of South Florida and entered the admissions office.

A woman in the admissions office told me that my academic adviser was mistaken and that I needed an AA degree to enroll for classes at their university?

Frustrated, confused, angry and hurt I drove back to the apartment complex and when I opened the door to my apartment, my brother and his girlfriend were sitting on my couch smoking a joint.

I couldn't take anymore of these idiots WITHIN my first "True Life" and shut the door, got back into my car and began driving, NOT knowing where I was going.

After some miles of driving, I saw a sign for an efficiency apartment for immediate occupancy.

I pulled into the parking lot and paid for a week.

It was one room with a shared kitchen and bathroom among two other rooms.

Spent the entire week lying in bed thinking?

Chapter and Sub Chapter 7 and Chapter 8 Moved Back to Ohio and Sub Chapter 8 Enrolled at Kent State Trumbull as well as Chapter and Sub Chapter 9 go here and hereafter but are found WITHIN The Silencer Project's Companion Book: The Poker Game Algorithm.

Here's a peek:

It was 1992 when Richard Jon Hassey graduated from then Edison Community College in Fort Myers, Florida with the ONLY computer programming degree the school ever issued with an analysis attached at the end of their standard programming degree, that is, Computer Programming and Analysis.

This same year Richard Jon Hassey wrote Activity 5.0 Security Application for the PC after moving back to Ohio and getting under a Patent Assistance Program with IBM.

In 1992 is when, IBM severed ties with Microsoft and went solo on their OS2 project.

It was 1994, when I was attending Georgia School of Technology, Georgia Tech, when IBM released OS2 Warp, that included the feature to launch Windows 3.1 as just another APPLICATION (APP).

An attorney said that Activity 6.0 Security Application (APP) for the PC copyright gives Burnt Store PC Corporation now BSPC Global Corporation its own GUI rights.

See this DuckDuckGo APP launcher?

That's the exact concept WITHIN Activity 5.0 and 6.0 Security Application for the PC uploaded to AOL's software library that Richard Jon Hassey obtained a copyright on back in the 90s.

The Activity 5.0 Application (now called APP) made Windows 3.1 just another APPLICATION (APP) to launch from a secure launching platform.

Chapter 10 – The Silencer Project
Stage 5

It's when the end user desires MORE that the configuration possibilities for the Television Commercial Silencer Electrical Wall Outlet Receptacle Tap become quite extensive. As a matter of truth, It would NOT be possible to cover all of the different audio device configuration possibilities in this application.

This compact unit should allow for the configuration of virtually any end user's desired audio setup.

(May also use Bluetooth dongle for additional options and functions: e.g., a 3.5mm Bluetooth dongle receiver inserted into the AUX port of the Television Commercial Silencer Electrical Wall Outlet Receptacle Tap will provide features such as: connecting one's smartphone wireless to the Television Commercial Silencer Electrical Wall Outlet Receptacle Tap allowing for playback of one's mp3 collection residing on one's phone, audio books or even online content from YouTube™).

Furthermore, don't forget that one's smartphone can also serve as the hand-held remote control for the Television Commercial Silencer Electrical Wall Outlet Receptacle Tap?

Many MORE configuration options will be included in the Stage 5 Manual. Please "stay tuned!"

P.S. To the manufacturer's, an RF modulator specially designed for the Television Commercial Silencer Electrical Wall Outlet Receptacle Tap will also provide NOT just e.g., YouTube™ audio but also video via the Television Commercial Silencer Electrical Wall Outlet Receptacle Tap.

Thus, YouTube™ audio and video e.g. could be presented to the End User during Television Commercial breaks. [In conclusion, utilizing a "Computer in a Box" such as a "Cubieboard ®" possibilities are extensive and the future of the Television Commercial Silencer Electrical Wall Outlet Receptacle Tap is bright!

Also, remember that if one's Television does NOT have built-in Bluetooth capabilities but has a headphone jack, one can plug a Bluetooth transmitter dongle into one's Television headphone jack or various other audio ports on the exterior of one's Television based on manufacturer?

In addition, even the oldest analog televisions that are still using analog to digital converter boxes can still benefit from the Television Commercial Silencer Electrical Wall Outlet Receptacle Tap via RCA cables and/or an RF modulator if need be?

There will be a solution for virtually every audio setup.

The unit is designed from the simple to the complex.

One can plug the unit in and listen to their television through the units' two internal stereo speakers or plug in their own external speakers?

If the end user chooses to use amplified speakers, they would simply plug the 3.5mm plug from their external speakers into the television audio OUT port on the front of the unit and the external amplified speaker's power cord into: addition, if the end user prefers to listen to their television through their television external audio system or home entertainment system, simply plug the respective power cord into: 2. Remote Controlled External Television Audio System Outlet?

The foregoing also applies to: 3. Remote Controlled External Radio/CD Player (BOOM BOX) etc. Audio System Outlet and 4. Remote Controlled External MP3/MP4 Player etc. Audio System Outlet?

The end user can also listen to their favorite MP3/MP4 music "Out of the Box" so to speak by simply plugging in a "FLASH" (USB) drive containing their own music into the front of the unit, if they prefer; or, as with the unit's internal stereo television audio speakers and internal radio, the end user can slide a switch on the front of the unit to turn off respectively each of the unit's internal audio devices entirely and plug in their own, in the respective: Remote Controlled External Audio System Outlet.

(Bluetooth speakers sold separately)

(May also use Bluetooth dongle for additional options and functions: e.g., an 3.5mm Bluetooth dongle receiver inserted into the AUX port of the Television Commercial Silencer Electrical Wall Outlet Receptacle Tap will provide features such as: connecting one's smart phone wirelessly to the Television Commercial Silencer Electrical Wall Outlet Receptacle Tap allowing for playback of one's mp3 collection residing on one's phone, audio books or even online content from YouTube™)?

Furthermore, don't forget that one's smartphone can also serve as the hand held remote control for the Television Commercial Silencer Electrical Wall Outlet Receptacle Tap?

Many MORE configuration options will be included in the Stage 5 Manual. Please "stay tuned!"

P.S. To the manufacturer's, an RF modulator specially designed for the Television Commercial Silencer Electrical Wall Outlet Receptacle Tap will also provide NOT just YouTube™ audio but also video via the Television Commercial Silencer Electrical Wall Outlet Receptacle Tap.

Thus, YouTube™ audio and video e.g. could be presented to the End User during Television Commercial breaks?

With your help, Hassey Solutions Television Commercial Silencer's "Packaging" will move from an

Electrical Work Box to its new Container as depicted in **Stage 5 User's Manual (Final Product)** that follows:

The new Container's design is similar to a standard multi-outlet electrical wall receptacle tap.

In truth, the official name of Hassey Solutions Final Product submitted to the United States Patent Office is:

"Television Commercial Silencer Electrical Wall Outlet Receptacle Tap.

It will be the same as buying similar items like multi-outlet wall taps or surge protectors in a blister pack that one simply plugs directly into the wall --ONLY this one's a **"SMART"** one!

U.S. Patent No. 10,249,996.

Hassey Solutions and Burnt Store PC Corporation are now BSPC Global Corporation, they'll now answer any questions:

BSPC Global Corporation
2600 E Seltice Way Ste A

PMB 2018

Post Falls, ID 83854
United States

Stage 5 User's Manual
(Final Product)
U.S. Patent No. 10,249,996.
Mock-up

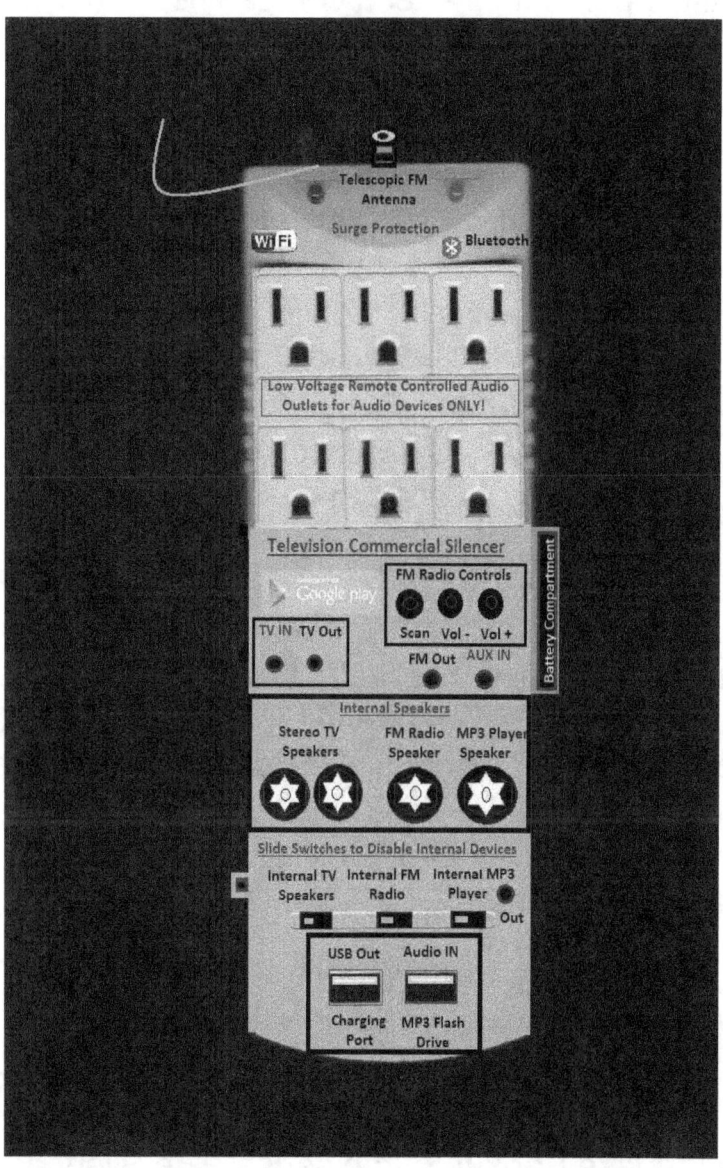

As of the Time-Toll of this completed manuscript, the Television Commercial Silencer Electrical Wall Outlet Receptacle Tap has NOT been manufactured.

In addition to a publishing company, BSPC Global Corporation is a tech company specializing in computer repair services, including custom built PCs and servers, as well as web hosting and data and web services.

BSPC Global Corporation is also a light 3D printing manufacturer, specifically to design a 3D model (.STL file) for the Television Commercial Silencer Electrical Wall Outlet Receptacle Tap electronics's enclosure US Patent NO. 10,249,996. Check-out Book III of The Domestic marine ® Tandem Book Writing and "Equational" and Engendered Poetry Series with parallel and recursive writing for all the details.

Once the .STL file is created of the Television Commercial Silencer Electrical Wall Outlet Receptacle Tap electronics's enclosure, the internal components can be assembled with a CubieBoard ® or Raspberry Pi ® at its CORE? -- Embedded technology and open-source hardware with a 3D printed electronics's enclosure, all from BSPC Global Corporation.

Additionally, a free downloadable user's manual, firmware and software updates will be available to all that purchase the Television Commercial Silencer Electrical Wall Outlet Receptacle Tap when available or who purchase Book III of the series, The Silencer Project: The Power of "The Night Sun" ☼ is total eclipse, or the joining of the sun ☼ with the moon, ☽

that is, The Birth of The "Night Star," * a new entity, and the first "Picture Painting" ☼ + ☽ = *.

Look for The Silencer Project's Companion Book, The Poker Game Algorithm for MORE on Computer Science.

See The Tandem Poetry Series. -- "Equational-Poetry," Engendered-Poetry, Invisilife-Poetry, and "Picture-Paintings" Poetry.

Stay informed at:

poetries-prior.com

truelifepoet.com

tandempoetry.com

YOU have reached the end of the

The Furthest and Nearest Night Stars:

The Birth of The Night Star ☼ + ☽ = *

Second Edition
Autographed

Imprint

Domestic marine, The ®

Author

Richard Jon Hassey

Publisher

Eating For "SELF" ™

Please consider other books from

BSPC Global Corporation
DBA
Burnt Store Publishers,
Hosting & Publishing

EFS Global Corporation,
DBA
Eating For "SELF," ™
DBA
True Life Poet
Publishing, Sales & Services
2600 E Seltice Way Ste A PMB 2013
Post Falls, Idaho, 83854

Richard Jon Hassey and

Nelfa Salise Hassey

Our Precious Anne just had a Freudian slip when Kleith asked her what did mommy tell YOU to do? Precious Anne said, I was talking to God, I mean Daddy.

When my two biological daughters were Precious' age their mother said that they thought I was God?
PRIOR to the last 50 years, "WE" have lived WITHIN an analog world but for this quite short time-toll now in "HISTORY," for a lifetime of The Every 50 Years-Old Flower, which I smelled, "WE" live WITHOUT God's world.
Does anyone understand the ramifications of living WITHOUT God's world?
What does one think the digital Gods teach our children?
I assured Precious Anne that I am NOT God and neither shall she find him in this digital world.
Moreover, your world shall fall and all of your God's are going straight to the black hole of hell.

The Furthest and Nearest Night Stars:

The Birth of The Night Star ☼ + ☽ = *

Second Edition
Autographed

by Richard Jon Hassey

ISBN 979-8-9900698-3-1

Edited by Burnt Store Publishers,

Hosting & Publishing.

Aces "ofLoves" ♥♣♦♠
acesofloves.com

Thank YOU for reading.

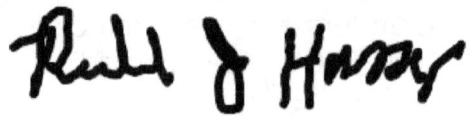

www.ingramcontent.com/pod-product-compliance
Lightning Source LLC
Chambersburg PA
CBHW060638130626
46555CB00002B/852